THE NEW TEMPLE SHAKESPEARE

Edited by M. R. Ridley, M.A.

THE WINTER'S TALE

by William Shakespeare

London: J. M. DENT & SONS LTD.
New York: E. P. DUTTON & CO. INC.

Editor's General Note

The Text. The editor has kept before him the aim of presenting to the modern reader the nearest possible approximation to what Shakespeare actually wrote. The text is therefore conservative, and is based on the earliest reliable printed text. But to avoid distraction (*a*) the spelling is modernised, and (*b*) a limited number of universally accepted emendations is admitted without comment. Where a Quarto text exists as well as the First Folio the passages which occur only in the Quarto are enclosed in square brackets [ ] and those which occur only in the Folio in brace brackets { }.

Scene Division. The rapid continuity of the Elizabethan curtainless production is lost by the 'traditional' scene divisions. Where there is an essential difference of place these scene divisions are retained. Where on the other hand the change of place is insignificant the scene division is indicated only by a space on the page. For ease of reference, however, the 'traditional' division is retained at the head of the page and in line numbering.

Notes. Passages on which there are notes are indicated by a † in the margin.

Punctuation adheres more closely than has been usual to the 'Elizabethan' punctuation of the early texts. It is often therefore more indicative of the way in which the lines were to be delivered than of their syntactical construction.

Glossaries are arranged on a somewhat novel principle, not alphabetically, but in the order in which the words or phrases occur. The editor is much indebted to Mr J. N. Bryson for his collaboration in the preparation of the glossaries.

Preface

The Text. The play appeared for the first time in print in the First Folio. The text there presented is unusually, and indeed almost suspiciously, free from obvious errors. It exhibits certain peculiarities which from the bibliographical point of view are of the highest interest, but as the consideration of them has small relevance to the determination of the text it would here be out of place. They perhaps point to the conclusion that the text was an 'assembled' text (*i.e.* one constructed, in the absence, or after the loss, of the complete MS., by piecing together the actors' parts), and almost certainly to the conclusion that the text was not an original MS. but (whether assembled or not) the work of a particular transcriber. The punctuation is elaborate, and there is an extensive (and usually significant and helpful) use of brackets.

Date of Composition. Here we are, so far as the *terminus ad quem* is concerned, on firm ground. The play was 'allowed, by Sir George Buc, who did not succeed Tylney as Master of the Revels till late 1610 (though it is true that he apparently acted for Tylney, who was a sick man, on occasions before that date). Dr Simon Forman saw the play in May 1611, and the careful and full account which he gives of the plot suggests that the play was new. How much earlier than this the play may have been in existence we have no external evidence to aid us in determining, but all the internal evidence of verse-texts and of 'temper' points to a late date. We shall not be far out in putting the play in 1610-11.

Sources. The main source is Greene's novel *Pandosto*, an extremely (and to modern taste surprisingly) popular work, which was first published in 1588 and ran through many editions. A detailed comparison of novel and play allows us to watch the operations of the lazy alchemist of genius. The main outline of the plot comes from Greene—the jealousy of Leontes, the banishing of Perdita, the oracle, the love of Perdita and Florizel, the ultimate recognition through the tokens kept by the old shepherd, and the reconciliation. But in the novel Hermione does in fact die at the news of her son's death, and Leontes after the recognition and general rejoicings somewhat unnecessarily kills himself in a fit of remorse (though in the novel he has more to be remorseful about, since Greene spends several weary pages in describing Leontes' passion for his yet unrecognised daughter, an episode which Shakespeare diminishes to one remark of Paulina's); a vast deal of dreary Euphuistic 'pastorality' is compressed in the play into two or three exquisite scenes; and Paulina, Autolycus, and Antigonus do not appear in the novel at all; nor indeed are they necessary for the movement of the play, though we should be sorry to lose them. In one point alone is the novel superior to the play, and that is in the growth of Leontes' jealousy, which in the novel is reasonably slow, and in the play so rapid as to be almost absurd. And while reading the novel for his play it is clear that every now and again Shakespeare's ear was caught by a phrase or two which he used. The clearest case of this verbal debt to Greene is perhaps the oracle itself which appears in Greene as follows (Shakespeare changes the names throughout the play; his Hermione is Bellaria, Egistus Polixenes, Leontes Pandosto, Camillo Franion): "Suspition is no proofe: iealousie is an unequall iudge: *Bellaria* is chast; *Egistus* blamelesse; *Franion* a true subiect; *Pandosto* treacherous: his babe an innocent, and the King shall live without an heire: if that which is lost be not founde." But we may also compare

' therefore if she were condemned without any further proofe, it was rigour, and not Law ' with

> *if I shall be condemn'd*
> *Upon surmises (all proofs sleeping else*
> *But what your jealousies awake) I tell you*
> *'Tis rigour and not law*

or ' If the devine powers be privy to humane actions (as no doubt they are) I hope my patience shall make fortune blushe ' with

> *if powers divine*
> *Behold our human actions (as they do)*
> *I doubt not then but innocence shall make*
> *False accusation blush, and tyranny*
> *Tremble at patience.*

or 'the heavenly Godes have sometimes earthly thoughtes : Neptune became a ram, Jupiter a Bul, Apollo a shepheard ' with

> *The gods themselves,*
> *Humbling their deities to love, have taken*
> *The shapes of beasts upon them : Jupiter*
> *Became a bull, and bellow'd ; the green Neptune*
> *A ram, and bleated ; and the fire-rob'd god*
> *Golden Apollo, a poor humble swain,*
> *As I seem now.*

Duration of Action. There are probably eight days represented on the stage, though by somewhat crowding events this extension could be somewhat shortened. There are only two main intervals, one for the emissaries to go to Delphi and return

(23 days) and the other between III and IV (indicated by 'Time'), (16 years).

Criticism. In this play Shakespeare was evidently attempting a dramatic *tour de force*, and in the opinion of many readers he only partially succeeded; indeed it may very reasonably be held that he did not succeed at all, but that some irrelevant excellences of poetry and characterisation are so magically lovely that they blind us to the failure. The truth, I think, is that the play as a whole is dramatically weak, and that of the two parts into which it falls the first is dramatically bad and the second dramatically excellent. In the first part Shakespeare is facing the capital difficulty which confronts any playwright setting out to dramatise a novel whose action extends over a considerable period of time. No doubt, if one throws the 'unities' to the winds, drama can represent a long period of time, but it can only do so by selecting a series of spaced episodes; what it cannot do (except to some extent by the clumsy method of reminiscence) is to show a development over a *continuous* long period, since in each episode the stage time must, within very narrow limits, coincide with the represented time. Hence the sudden and frantic blazing up of Leontes' jealousy is improbable to the point of absurdity, and, seeing that it is the mainspring of the whole action, its falsity tinges the whole of the first three acts with unreality. Leontes is too bad, almost too silly, to be true, and not all Shakespeare's dramatic skill, not Mamillius, not the pungent and fierce loyalty of Paulina, not the calm pride of Hermione, can really persuade us that the first half of the play is more than a rather unskilful introduction to the second half. But when, on the insecure bridge of Time's feebly obscure (and, one hopes, non-Shakespearean) couplets, we have crossed the gap of sixteen years, we have forgotten the false premises, we are in a world where emotions are real again and not Fletcherian, and the drama moves coherently to its end.

Of the various problems presented by Shakespeare's last plays, how far they are 'plays of reconcilement,' or 'the evening sunlight after storm,' or merely the work of a man too tired to be tragic, though I hope to say something in the companion volume to this edition, I propose to say nothing here, since they can be studied only in relation to all the plays taken together. I will only suggest that if any reader of this play will, immediately on the head of it, read *Pericles, Cymbeline,* and *The Tempest* he will have gone far towards an understanding of Shakespeare.

Hazlitt.—We wonder that Mr Pope should have entertained doubts of the genuineness of this play. He was, we suppose, shocked (as a certain critic suggests) at the Chorus, Time, leaping over sixteen years with his crutch between the third and fourth act, and at Antigonus's landing with the infant Perdita on the sea-coast of Bohemia. These slips or blemishes, however, do not prove it not to be Shakespear's; for he was as likely to fall into them as any body; but we do not know any body but himself who could produce the beauties. The *stuff* of which the tragic passion is composed, the romantic sweetness, the comic humour, are evidently his. Even the crabbed and tortuous style of the speeches of Leontes, reasoning on his own jealousy, beset with doubts and fears, and entangled more and more in the thorny labyrinth, bears every mark of Shakespear's peculiar manner of conveying the painful struggle of different thoughts and feelings, labouring for utterance, and almost strangled in the birth. . . .

The character of Hermione is as much distinguished by its saint-like resignation and patient forbearance, as that of Paulina is by her zealous and spirited remonstrances against the injustice done to the queen, and by her devoted attachment to her misfortunes. Hermione's restoration to her husband and her child, after her long separation from them, is as affecting in itself as it is striking in the representation. Camillo, and the old shepherd and his son, are subordinate but not uninteresting instruments in the development of the plot, and though last, not least, comes Autolycus, a very pleasant, thriving rogue; and (what is the best feather in the cap of all knavery) he escapes with impunity in the end.

Swinburne.[1]—The wild wind of the *Winter's Tale* at its opening would seem to blow us back into a wintrier world indeed. And to the very end I must confess that I have in me so much of the spirit of Rachel weeping in Ramah as will not be comforted because Mamillius is not. It is well for those whose hearts are light enough, to take perfect comfort even in the substitution of his sister Perdita for the boy who died of 'thoughts high for one so tender.' Even the beautiful suggestion that Shakespeare as he wrote had in mind his own dead little son still fresh and living at his heart can hardly add more than a touch of additional tenderness to our perfect and piteous delight in him. And even in her daughter's embrace it seems hard if his mother should have utterly forgotten the little voice that had only time to tell her just eight words of that ghost story which neither she nor we were ever to hear ended. Any one but Shakespeare would have sought to make pathetic profit out of the child by the easy means of showing him if but once again as changed and stricken to the death for want of his mother and

[1] Reprinted by permission of the Publishers, W. Heinemann Ltd., from *A Study of Shakespeare.*

fear for her and hunger and thirst at his little high heart for the
sight and touch of her: Shakespeare only could find a better way,
a subtler and a deeper chord to strike, by giving us our last glimpse
of him as he laughed and chattered with her " past enduring," to
the shameful neglect of those ladies in the natural blueness of whose
eyebrows as well as their noses he so stoutly declined to believe.
And at the very end (as aforesaid) it may be that we remember him
all the better because the father whose jealousy killed him and the
mother for love of whom he died would seem to have forgotten
the little brave sweet spirit with all its truth of love and tender
sense of shame as perfectly and unpardonably as Shakespeare
himself at the close of *King Lear* would seem to have forgotten one
who never had forgotten Cordelia.

But yet—and here for once the phrase abhorred by Cleopatra
does not " allay the good " but only the bad " precedence "—if
ever amends could be made for such unnatural show of seeming
forgetfulness (" out on the seeming !   I will write against it "—or
would, had I not written enough already), the poet most assuredly
has made such amends here.   At the sunrise of Perdita beside
Florizel it seems as if the snows of sixteen winters had melted all
together into the splendour of one unutterable spring.   They
" smell April and May " in a sweeter sense than it could be said of
" young Master Fenton ": " nay, which is more," as his friend
and champion Mistress Quickly might have added to mine host's
commendatory remark, they speak all April and May; because
April is in him as naturally as May in her, by just so many years'
difference before the Mayday of her birth as went to make up her
dead brother's little lot of living breath, which in Beaumont's most
lovely and Shakespeare-worthy phrase " was not a life; was but a
piece of childhood thrown away."   Nor can I be content to find

xiii

no word of old affection for Autolycus, who lived, as we may not
doubt, though but a hint or promise be vouchsafed us for all assur-
ance that he lived by favour of his " good masters " once more to
serve Prince Florizel and wear three-pile for as much of his time
as it might please him to put on " robes " like theirs that were
" gentlemen born," and had " been so any time these four hours."
And yet another and a graver word must be given with all reverence
to the " grave and good Paulina," whose glorious fire of godlike
indignation was as warmth and cordial to the innermost heart
while yet bruised and wrung for the yet fresh loss of Mamillius.

THE WINTER'S TALE

DRAMATIS PERSONÆ

LEONTES, *king of Sicilia.*

MAMILLIUS, *young prince of Sicilia.*

CAMILLO,
ANTIGONUS, } *Four Lords of Sicilia.*
CLEOMENES,
DION,

POLIXENES, *king of Bohemia.*

FLORIZEL, *prince of Bohemia.*

ARCHIDAMUS, *a Lord of Bohemia.*

Old Shepherd, *reputed father of Perdita.*

Clown, *his son.*

AUTOLYCUS, *a rogue.*

A Mariner.

A Gaoler.

HERMIONE, *queen to Leontes.*

PERDITA, *daughter to Leontes and Hermione.*

PAULINA, *wife to Antigonus.*

EMILIA, *a lady attending on Hermione.*

MOPSA, } *Shepherdesses.*
DORCAS,

Other Lords and Gentlemen, Ladies, Officers, **and**
Servants, Shepherds, and Shepherdesses.

Time, as Chorus.

SCENE: *Partly in Sicilia, and partly in Bohemia.*

THE WINTER'S TALE

Act First

SCENES I AND II

Leontes' palace

Enter Camillo and Archidamus

Arc. If you shall chance, Camillo, to visit Bohemia, on the like occasion whereon my services are now on foot, you shall see, as I have said, great difference betwixt our Bohemia and your Sicilia.

Cam. I think, this coming summer, the King of Sicilia means to pay Bohemia the visitation which he justly owes him.

Arc. Wherein our entertainment shall shame us ; we will be justified in our loves ; for indeed—

Cam. Beseech you,—

Arc. Verily I speak it in the freedom of my knowledge : we cannot with such magnificence—in so rare—I know not what to say. We will give you sleepy drinks, that your senses, unintelligent of our insufficience, may, though they cannot praise us, as little accuse us.

Cam. You pay a great deal too dear for what's given freely.

Arc. Believe me, I speak as my understanding instructs me, and as mine honesty puts it to utterance. 20

Cam. Sicilia cannot show himself over-kind to Bohemia. They were train'd together in their childhoods; and there rooted betwixt them then such an affection, which cannot choose but branch now. Since their more mature dignities, and royal necessities, made separation of their society, their encounters, though not personal, have been royally attorneyed with interchange of gifts, letters, loving embassies, that they have seem'd to be together, though absent; shook hands, as over a vast; and embrac'd as it 30 were from the ends of opposed winds. The heavens continue their loves!

Arc. I think there is not in the world either malice or matter to alter it. You have an unspeakable comfort of your young prince Mamillius: it is a gentleman of the greatest promise that ever came into my note.

Cam. I very well agree with you in the hopes of him: it is a gallant child; one that indeed physics the subject, makes old hearts fresh: they that went on crutches ere he was born desire yet their life, to 40 see him a man.

2

Arc. Would they else be content to die ?

Cam. Yes ; if there were no other excuse why they should
desire to live.

Arc. If the king had no son, they would desire to live on
crutches till he had one.   *Exeunt*

*Enter Leontes, Hermione, Mamillius, Polixenes, Camillo,
and Attendants*

Pol. Nine changes of the watery star hath been
The shepherd's note since we have left our throne
Without a burthen : time as long again
Would be fill'd up, my brother, with our thanks,
And yet we should, for perpetuity,
Go hence in debt : and therefore, like a cipher,
Yet standing in rich place, I multiply
With one ' We thank you,' many thousands moe
That go before it.

Leo.   Stay your thanks a while,
And pay them when you part.

Pol.   Sir, that 's to-morrow. 10
I am question'd by my fears, of what may chance   †
Or breed upon our absence, that may blow

3

    (No sneaping winds at home) to make us say
    'This is put forth too truly:' besides, I have stay'd
    To tire your royalty.

Leo.   We are tougher, brother,
    Than you can put us to 't.

Pol.   No longer stay.

Leo. One seven-night longer.

Pol.   Very sooth, to-morrow.

Leo. We'll part the time between's, then: and in that
    I'll no gainsaying.

Pol.   Press me not, beseech you, so.
    There is no tongue that moves, none, none i' the
        world,   20
    So soon as yours could win me: so it should now,
    Were there necessity in your request, although
    'Twere needful I denied it. My affairs
    Do even drag me homeward: which to hinder
    Were (in your love) a whip to me; my stay
    To you a charge and trouble: to save both,
    Farewell, our brother.

Leo.   Tongue-tied our queen? speak you.

Her. I had·thought, sir, to have held my peace, until
    You had drawn oaths from him not to stay. You,
        sir,
    Charge him too coldly. Tell him, you are sure   30

4

       All in Bohemia's well; this satisfaction
       The by-gone day proclaim'd : say this to him,
       He's beat from his best ward.

Leo.   Well said, Hermione.

Her. To tell, he longs to see his son, were strong :
       But let him say so then, and let him go ;
       But let him swear so, and he shall not stay,
       We'll thwack him hence with distaffs.
       Yet of your royal presence I'll adventure
       The borrow of a week.   When at Bohemia
       You take my lord, I'll give him my commission   40
       To let him there a month behind the gest
       Prefix'd for 's parting : yet, good deed, Leontes,
       I love thee not a jar o' the clock behind
       What lady she her lord.   You'll stay ?

Pol.   No, madam.

Her. Nay, but you will ?

Pol.   I may not, verily.

Her. Verily ?
       You put me off with limber vows ; but I,
       Though you would seek to unsphere the stars with
          oaths,
       Should yet say ' Sir, no going.'   Verily,
       You shall not go : a lady's ' Verily ' is   50
       As potent as a lord's.   Will you go yet ?

Force me to keep you as a prisoner,
Not like a guest; so you shall pay your fees
When you depart, and save your thanks.   How say
    you?
My prisoner? or my guest? by your dread 'Verily,'
One of them you shall be.

Pol.   Your guest, then, madam:
To be your prisoner should import offending;
Which is for me less easy to commit
Than you to punish.

Her.   Not your gaoler, then,
But your kind hostess.   Come, I'll question you   60
Of my lord's tricks, and yours, when you were boys:
You were pretty lordings then?

Pol.   We were, fair queen,
Two lads that thought there was no more behind,
But such a day to-morrow as to-day,
And to be boy eternal.

Her   Was not my lord
The verier wag o' the two?

Pol. We were as twinn'd lambs, that did frisk i' the sun,
And bleat the one at the other: what we chang'd
Was innocence for innocence; we knew not
The doctrine of ill-doing, nor dream'd   70
That any did.   Had we pursued that life,

6

And our weak spirits ne'er been higher rear'd
With stronger blood, we should have answer'd heaven
Boldly ' not guilty ; ' the imposition clear'd   †
Hereditary ours.

Her.   By this we gather
You have tripp'd since.

Pol.   O my most sacred lady,
Temptations have since then been born to 's : for
In those unfledg'd days was my wife a girl ;
Your precious self had then not cross'd the eyes
Of my young play-fellow.

Her.   Grace to boot !   80
Of this make no conclusion, lest you say
Your queen and I are devils : yet go on ;
The offences we have made you do we 'll answer,
If you first sinn'd with us ; and that with us
You did continue fault ; and that you slipp'd not
With any but with us.

Leo.   Is he won yet ?

Her. He 'll stay, my lord.

Leo.   At my request he would not.
Hermione, my dearest, thou never spok'st
To better purpose.

Her.   Never ?

Leo.   Never, but once.

Her. What ? have I twice said well ? when was 't before ?   90
    I prithee tell me ; cram 's with praise, and make 's
    As fat as tame things : one good deed, dying tongueless,
    Slaughters a thousand waiting upon that.
    Our praises are our wages : you may ride 's
    With one soft kiss a thousand furlongs, ere
    With spur we heat an acre.   But to the goal :   †
    My last good deed was to entreat his stay :
    What was my first ? it has an elder sister,
    Or I mistake you : O, would her name were Grace !
    But once before I spoke to the purpose ? when ?   100
    Nay, let me have 't ; I long.

Leo.   Why, that was when
    Three crabbed months had sour'd themselves to death,
    Ere I could make thee open thy white hand,
    And clap thyself my love : then didst thou utter
    ' I am yours for ever.'

Her.   'Tis Grace indeed.
    Why, lo you now, I have spoke to the purpose twice :
    The one for ever earn'd a royal husband ;
    The other for some while a friend.

Leo.   (*aside*) Too hot, too hot !
    To mingle friendship far is mingling bloods.
    I have tremor cordis on me : my heart dances,   110
    But not for joy ; not joy.   This entertainment

May a free face put on ; derive a liberty
From heartiness, from bounty, fertile bosom,
And well become the agent ; 't may, I grant ;
But to be paddling palms, and pinching fingers,
As now they are, and making practis'd smiles,
As in a looking-glass ; and then to sigh, as 'twere
The mort o' the deer ; O, that is entertainment
My bosom likes not, nor my brows !   Mamillius,
Art thou my boy ?

Mam.   Ay, my good lord.

Leo.   I' fecks !   120

Why, that 's my bawcock.   What, hast smutch'd thy
      nose ?
They say it is a copy out of mine.   Come, captain,
We must be neat ; not neat, but cleanly, captain :
And yet the steer, the heifer, and the calf
Are all call'd neat.—Still virginalling
Upon his palm ?—How now, you wanton calf !
Art thou my calf ?

Mam.   Yes, if you will, my lord.

Leo. Thou want'st a rough pash and the shoots that I have,
To be full like me : yet they say we are
Almost as like as eggs ; women say so,   130
That will say any thing : but were they false
As o'er-dyed blacks, as wind, as waters, false

9

As dice are to be wish'd by one that fixes
No bourn 'twixt his and mine, yet were it true
To say this boy were like me.   Come, sir page,
Look on me with your welkin eye : sweet villain,
Most dear'st! my collop! Can thy dam?—may 't be?
Affection? thy intention stabs the centre :   †
Thou dost make possible things not so held,
Communicat'st with dreams ;—how can this be?—   140
With what 's unreal thou coactive art,
And fellow'st nothing : then 'tis very credent
Thou mayst co-join with something ; and thou dost,
And that beyond commission, and I find it,
And that to the infection of my brains
And hardening of my brows.

Pol.   What means Sicilia?

Her. He something seems unsettled.

Pol.   How, my lord?

Leo. What cheer? how is 't with you, best brother?

Her.   You look
As if you held a brow of much distraction :
Are you mov'd, my lord?

Leo.   No, in good earnest.   150
How sometimes nature will betray its folly,
Its tenderness, and make itself a pastime
To harder bosoms ! Looking on the lines

Of my boy's face, methoughts I did recoil
Twenty-three years, and saw myself unbreech'd,
In my green velvet coat, my dagger muzzled
Lest it should bite its master, and so prove,
As ornaments oft do, too dangerous :
How like, methought, I then was to this kernel,
This squash, this gentleman.   Mine honest friend,   160
Will you take eggs for money ?

Mam. No, my lord, I 'll fight.

Leo. You will ! why, happy man be 's dole !   My brother,
Are you so fond of your young prince, as we
Do seem to be of ours ?

Pol.   If at home, sir,
He 's all my exercise, my mirth, my matter :
Now my sworn friend, and then mine enemy ;
My parasite, my soldier, statesman, all :
He makes a July's day short as December,
And with his varying childness cures in me   170
Thoughts that would thick my blood.

Leo.   So stands this squire
Offic'd with me : we two will walk, my lord,
And leave you to your graver steps.   Hermione,
How thou lov'st us, show in our brother's welcome ;
Let what is dear in Sicily be cheap :
Next to thyself and my young rover, he 's

      Apparent to my heart.

Her.   If you would seek us,
      We are yours i' the garden : shall 's attend you there ?

Leo. To your own bents dispose you : you 'll be found,
      Be you beneath the sky.   *(aside)* I am angling now,   180
      Though you perceive me not how I give line.
      Go to, go to !
      How she holds up the neb, the bill to him !
      And arms her with the boldness of a wife
      To her allowing husband !

                  Exeunt Polixenes, Hermione, and Attendants
                    Gone already !
      Inch-thick, knee-deep, o'er head and ears a fork'd one !
      Go, play, boy, play : thy mother plays, and I
      Play too ; but so disgrac'd a part, whose issue
      Will hiss me to my grave : contempt and clamour
      Will be my knell.   Go, play, boy, play.   There have
          been,   190
      (Or I am much deceived) cuckolds ere now,
      And many a man there is (even at this present,
      Now, while I speak this) holds his wife by the arm,
      That little thinks she has been sluic'd in 's absence
      And his pond fish'd by his next neighbour, by
      Sir Smile, his neighbour : nay, there 's comfort in 't,
      Whiles other men have gates, and those gates open'd,

As mine, against their will.   Should all despair
That have revolted wives, the tenth of mankind
Would hang themselves.   Physic for't there's none; 200
It is a bawdy planet, that will strike
Where 'tis predominant; and 'tis powerful, think it,
From east, west, north and south, be it concluded,
No barricado for a belly; know 't;
It will let in and out the enemy
With bag and baggage : many thousand on 's
Have the disease, and feel 't not.   How now, boy ?

Mam. I am like you, they say.

Leo.   Why, that 's some comfort.
What, Camillo there ?

Cam. Ay, my good lord.   210

Leo. Go play, Mamillius ; thou 'rt an honest man.

                                        Exit Mamillius

Camillo, this great sir will yet stay longer.

Cam. You had much ado to make his anchor hold :
When you cast out, it still came home.

Leo.   Didst note it ?

Cam. He would not stay at your petitions ; made
His business more material.

Leo.   Didst perceive it ?
   (*aside*) They 're here with me already ; whispering,
        rounding

13

' Sicilia is a so-forth : ' 'tis far gone,
When I shall gust it last.—How came 't, Camillo,
That he did stay ?

Cam.   At the good queen's entreaty.   220

Leo. At the queen's be 't : ' good ' should be pertinent ;
But, so it is, it is not.   Was this taken
By any understanding pate but thine ?
For thy conceit is soaking, will draw in
More than the common blocks : but noted, is 't,
But of the finer natures ? by some severals
Of head-piece extraordinary ? lower messes
Perchance are to this business purblind ? say.

Cam. Business, my lord ?   I think most understand
Bohemia stays here longer.

Leo.   Ha ?

Cam.   Stays here longer.   230

Leo. Ay, but why ?

Cam. To satisfy your highness, and the entreaties
Of our most gracious mistress.

Leo.   Satisfy ?
The entreaties of your mistress ? satisfy ?
Let that suffice.   I have trusted thee, Camillo,
With all the nearest things to my heart, as well
My chamber-counsels, wherein, priest-like, thou
Hast cleans'd my bosom ; I from thee departed

Thy penitent reform'd : but we have been
Deceiv'd in thy integrity, deceiv'd   240
In that which seems so.

Cam.   Be it forbid, my lord !

Leo. To bide upon 't, thou art not honest ; or,
  If thou inclin'st that way, thou art a coward,
  Which hoxes honesty behind, restraining
  From course requir'd ; or else thou must be counted
  A servant, grafted in my serious trust,
  And therein negligent ; or else a fool
  That seest a game play'd home, the rich stake drawn,
  And tak'st it all for jest.

Cam.   My gracious lord,
  I may be negligent, foolish, and fearful ;   250
  In every one of these no man is free,
  But that his negligence, his folly, fear,
  Among the infinite doings of the world,
  Sometime puts forth.   In your affairs, my lord,
  If ever I were wilful-negligent,
  It was my folly ; if industriously
  I play'd the fool, it was my negligence,
  Not weighing well the end ; if ever fearful
  To do a thing, where I the issue doubted,
  Whereof the execution did cry out   260
  Against the non-performance, 'twas a fear

Which oft infects the wisest : these, my lord,
Are such allow'd infirmities that honesty
Is never free of.   But, beseech your Grace,
Be plainer with me, let me know my trespass
By its own visage : if I then deny it,
'Tis none of mine.

Leo.   Ha' not you seen, Camillo ?
(But that's past doubt ; you have, or your eye-glass
Is thicker than a cuckold's horn,) or heard ?
(For to a vision so apparent rumour   27c
Cannot be mute) or thought ? (for cogitation
Resides not in that man that does not think)
My wife is slippery ?   If thou wilt confess,
Or else be impudently negative,
To have nor eyes, nor ears, nor thought, then say
My wife's a hobby-horse, deserves a name
As rank as any flax-wench that puts to
Before her troth-plight : say 't, and justify 't.

*Cam.*I would not be a stander-by to hear
My sovereign mistress clouded so, without   28c
My present vengeance taken : 'shrew my heart,
You never spoke what did become you less
Than this ; which to reiterate were sin
As deep as that, though true.

Leo.   Is whispering nothing ?

16

Is leaning cheek to cheek ? is meeting noses ?
Kissing with inside lip ? stopping the career
Of laughter with a sigh (a note infallible
Of breaking honesty) ? horsing foot on foot ?
Skulking in corners ? wishing clocks more swift ?
Hours, minutes ? noon, midnight ? and all eyes   290
Blind with the pin and web but theirs ; theirs only,
That would unseen be wicked ? is this nothing ?
Why, then the world, and all that 's in 't, is nothing,
The covering sky is nothing, Bohemia nothing,
My wife is nothing, nor nothing have these nothings,
If this be nothing.

Cam.   Good my lord, be cur'd
Of this diseas'd opinion, and betimes,
For 'tis most dangerous.

Leo.   Say it be, 'tis true.

Cam. No, no, my lord.

Leo.   It is ; you lie, you lie :
I say thou liest, Camillo, and I hate thee,   300
Pronounce thee a gross lout, a mindless slave,
Or else a hovering temporizer, that
Canst with thine eyes at once see good and evil,
Inclining to them both : were my wife's liver
Infected as her life, she would not live
The running of one glass.

Cam.   Who does infect her?

Leo. Why, he that wears her like her medal, hanging
    About his neck, Bohemia, who, if I
    Had servants true about me, that bare eyes
    To see alike mine honour as their profits,   310
    (Their own particular thrifts) they would do that
    Which should undo more doing: ay, and thou,
    His cupbearer, whom I from meaner form
    Have bench'd, and rear'd to worship, who mayst see
    Plainly, as heaven sees earth and earth sees heaven,
    How I am galled, mightst bespice a cup,
    To give mine enemy a lasting wink;
    Which draught to me were cordial.

Cam.   Sir, my lord,
    I could do this, and that with no rash potion,
    But with a lingering dram, that should not work   320
    Maliciously like poison: but I cannot
    Believe this crack to be in my dread mistress,
    So sovereignly being honourable.
    I have lov'd thee,—

Leo.   Make that thy question, and go rot!
    Dost think I am so muddy, so unsettled,
    To appoint myself in this vexation; sully
    The purity and whiteness of my sheets,
    (Which to preserve is sleep, which being spotted

Is goads, thorns, nettles, tails of wasps ;)
Give scandal to the blood o' the prince my son,   330
(Who I do think is mine, and love as mine)
Without ripe moving to 't ?   Would I do this ?
Could man so blench ?

Cam.   I must believe you, sir :
I do ; and will fetch off Bohemia for 't ;
Provided that, when he 's remov'd, your highness
Will take again your queen as yours at first,
Even for your son's sake, and thereby for sealing
The injury of tongues in courts and kingdoms
Known and allied to yours.

Leo.   Thou dost advise me
Even so as I mine own course have set down :   340
I 'll give no blemish to her honour, none.

Cam. My lord,
Go then ; and with a countenance as clear
As friendship wears at feasts, keep with Bohemia
And with your queen.   I am his cupbearer :
If from me he have wholesome beverage,
Account me not your servant.

Leo.   This is all :
Do 't, and thou hast the one half of my heart ;
Do 't not, thou splitt'st thine own.

Cam.   I 'll do 't, my lord.

19

Leo. I will seem friendly, as thou hast advis'd me.   *Exit* 350

Cam. O miserable lady! But, for me,
What case stand I in? I must be the poisoner
Of good Polixenes, and my ground to do 't
Is the obedience to a master, one
Who, in rebellion with himself, will have
All that are his, so too. To do this deed,
Promotion follows. If I could find example
Of thousands that had struck anointed kings
And flourish'd after, I 'ld not do 't; but since
Nor brass, nor stone, nor parchment bears not one, 360
Let villany itself forswear 't. I must
Forsake the court: to do 't, or no, is certain
To me a break-neck. Happy star reign now!
Here comes Bohemia.

Re-enter Polixenes

Pol.   This is strange: methinks
My favour here begins to warp. Not speak?
Good day, Camillo.

Cam.   Hail, most royal sir!

Pol. What is the news i' the court?

Cam.   None rare, my lord.

Pol. The king hath on him such a countenance
As he had lost some province, and a region
Lov'd as he loves himself: even now I met him 370

With customary compliment, when he,
Wafting his eyes to the contrary, and falling
A lip of much contempt, speeds from me, and
So leaves me, to consider what is breeding,
That changes thus his manners.

Cam. I dare not know, my lord.

Pol. How, dare not? do not? Do you know, and dare
     not?
Be intelligent to me : 'tis thereabouts ;
For, to yourself, what you do know, you must,
And cannot say, you dare not. Good Camillo,   380
Your chang'd complexions are to me a mirror
Which shows me mine chang'd too ; for I must be
A party in this alteration, finding
Myself thus alter'd with 't.

Cam.   There is a sickness
Which puts some of us in distemper, but
I cannot name the disease, and it is caught
Of you, that yet are well.

Pol.   How caught of me?
Make me not sighted like the basilisk :
I have look'd on thousands, who have sped the better
By my regard, but kill'd none so. Camillo,—   390
As you are certainly a gentleman, thereto
Clerk-like experienc'd, which no less adorns

Our gentry than our parents' noble names,
In whose success we are gentle,—I beseech you,
If you know aught which does behove my knowledge
Thereof to be inform'd, imprison 't not
In ignorant concealment.

Cam.   I may not answer.

Pol. A sickness caught of me, and yet I well ?
I must be answer'd.   Dost thou hear, Camillo,
I conjure thee, by all the parts of man   400
Which honour does acknowledge, whereof the least
Is not this suit of mine, that thou declare
What incidency thou dost guess of harm
Is creeping toward me ; how far off, how near,
Which way to be prevented, if to be ;
If not, how best to bear it.

Cam.   Sir, I will tell you,
Since I am charged in honour, and by him
That I think honourable : therefore mark my counsel,
Which must be ev'n as swiftly follow'd as
I mean to utter it ; or both yourself, and me,   410
Cry lost, and so good night !

Pol.   On, good Camillo.

Cam. I am appointed him to murder you.

Pol. By whom, Camillo ?

Cam.   By the king.

22

Pol.   For what ?

Cam. He thinks, nay, with all confidence he swears,
    As he had seen 't, or been an instrument
    To vice you to 't, that you have touch'd his queen
    Forbiddenly.

Pol.   O then, my best blood turn
    To an infected jelly, and my name
    Be yok'd with his that did betray the Best !
    Turn then my freshest reputation to   420
    A savour that may strike the dullest nostril
    Where I arrive, and my approach be shunn'd,
    Nay, hated too, worse than the great'st infection
    That e'er was heard or read !

Cam.   Swear his thought over
    By each particular star in heaven, and
    By all their influences ; you may as well
    Forbid the sea for to obey the moon,
    As or by oath remove or counsel shake
    The fabric of his folly, whose foundation
    Is pil'd upon his faith, and will continue   430
    The standing of his body.

Pol.   How should this grow ?

Cam. I know not : but I am sure 'tis safer to
    Avoid what 's grown, than question how 'tis born.
    If therefore you dare trust my honesty,

23

That lies enclosed in this trunk, which you
Shall bear along impawn'd, away to-night !
Your followers I will whisper to the business,
And will by twos and threes, at several posterns,
Clear them o' the city.   For myself, I 'll put
My fortunes to your service, which are here   440
By this discovery lost.   Be not uncertain,
For, by the honour of my parents, I
Have utter'd truth : which if you seek to prove,
I dare not stand by ; nor shall you be safer
Than one condemn'd by the king's own mouth, thereon
His execution sworn.

Pol.   I do believe thee :
I saw his heart in 's face.   Give me thy hand :
Be pilot to me, and thy places shall
Still neighbour mine.   My ships are ready, and
My people did expect my hence departure   450
Two days ago.   This jealousy
Is for a precious creature : as she 's rare,
Must it be great ; and, as his person 's mighty,
Must it be violent ; and as he does conceive
He is dishonour'd by a man which ever
Profess'd to him, why, his revenges must
In that be made more bitter.   Fear o'ershades me :
Good expedition be my friend, and comfort   †

24

The gracious queen, part of his theme, but nothing
Of his ill-ta'en suspicion ! Come, Camillo ;   460
I will respect thee as a father if
Thou bear'st my life off ; hence, let us avoid.
*Cam.*It is in mine authority to command
The keys of all the posterns : please your highness
To take the urgent hour. Come sir, away. *Exeunt*

Act Second

SCENE I

A room in Leontes' palace

Enter Hermione, Mamillius, and Ladies

Her. Take the boy to you : he so troubles me,
'Tis past enduring.
1.L.   Come, my gracious lord,
Shall I be your playfellow ?
Mam.   No, I 'll none of you.
1.L. Why, my sweet lord ?
*Mam.*You 'll kiss me hard, and speak to me as if
I were a baby still. I love you better.
2.L. And why so, my lord ?

Mam.   Not for because
    Your brows are blacker ; yet black brows, they say,
    Become some women best, so that there be not
    Too much hair there, but in a semicircle,   **10**
    Or a half-moon, made with a pen.
2.L.   Who taught this ?
Mam. I learn'd it out of women's faces.   Pray now
    What colour are your eyebrows ?
1.L.   Blue, my lord.
Mam. Nay, that 's a mock : I have seen a lady's nose
    That has been blue, but not her eyebrows.
1.L.   Hark ye,
    The queen your mother rounds apace : we shall
    Present our services to a fine new prince
    One of these days, and then you 'ld wanton with us,
    If we would have you.
2.L.   She is spread of late
    Into a goodly bulk : good time encounter her !   **20**
Her. What wisdom stirs amongst you ?   Come, Sir, now
    I am for you again : pray you, sit by us,
    And tell 's a tale.
Mam.   Merry, or sad, shall 't be ?
Her. As merry as you will.
Mam. A sad tale 's best for winter : I have one
    Of sprites, and goblins.

Her.   Let 's have that, good sir.
Come on, sit down, come on, and do your best
To fright me with your sprites ; you 're powerful
    at it.

Mam. There was a man—

Her.   Nay, come, sit down ; then on.

Mam. Dwelt by a churchyard : I will tell it softly,   30
Yond crickets shall not hear it.

Her.   Come on, then,
And give 't me in mine ear.

        Enter Leontes, with Antigonus, Lords, and others

Leo. Was he met there ? his train ? Camillo with him ?

1.L. Behind the tuft of pines I met them ; never
Saw I men scour so on their way : I ey'd them
Even to their ships.

Leo.   How blest am I
In my just censure, in my true opinion !
Alack, for lesser knowledge, how accurs'd
In being so blest !   There may be in the cup
A spider steep'd, and one may drink, depart,   40
And yet partake no venom (for his knowledge
Is not infected :) but if one present
The abhorr'd ingredient to his eye, make known
How he hath drunk, he cracks his gorge, his sides,
With violent hefts.   I have drunk, and seen the spider.

Camillo was his help in this, his pandar :
There is a plot against my life, my crown ;
All 's true that is mistrusted : that false villain,
Whom I employ'd, was pre-employ'd by him :
He has discover'd my design, and I   50
Remain a pinch'd thing ; yea, a very trick
For them to play at will.   How came the posterns
So easily open ?

1.L.   By his great authority,
Which often hath no less prevail'd than so
On your command.

Leo.   I know 't too well.
Give me the boy, I am glad you did not nurse him :
Though he does bear some signs of me, yet you
Have too much blood in him.

Her.   What is this ? sport ?

Leo. Bear the boy hence, he shall not come about her,
Away with him, and let her sport herself   60
With that she 's big with, for 'tis Polixenes
Has made thee swell thus.

Her.   But I 'ld say he had not ;
And I 'll be sworn you would believe my saying,
Howe'er you lean to the nayward.

Leo.   You, my lords,
Look on her, mark her well ; be but about

To say 'she is a goodly lady,' and
The justice of your hearts will thereto add
' 'Tis pity she's not honest, honourable : '
Praise her but for this her without-door form,
(Which on my faith deserves high speech) and straight   70
The shrug, the hum, or ha (these pretty brands
That calumny doth use ; O, I am out,
That mercy does, for calumny will sear
Virtue itself :) these shrugs, these hums, and ha's,
When you have said ' she's goodly,' come between
Ere you can say ' she's honest : ' but be 't known,
(From him that has most cause to grieve it should be)
She's an adulteress.

Her.   Should a villain say so,
The most replenish'd villain in the world,
He were as much more villain : you, my lord,   80
Do but mistake.

Leo.   You have mistook, my lady,
Polixenes for Leontes : O thou thing !
Which I 'll not call a creature of thy place,
Lest barbarism, making me the precedent,
Should a like language use to all degrees,
And mannerly distinguishment leave out
Betwixt the prince and beggar : I have said
She's an adulteress, I have said with whom :

More ; she 's a traitor, and Camillo is
A federary with her, and one that knows,   90
What she should shame to know herself,
But with her most vile principal, that she 's
A bed-swerver, even as bad as those
That vulgars give bold'st titles ; ay, and privy
To this their late escape.

Her.   No, by my life,
Privy to none of this.   How will this grieve you,
When you shall come to clearer knowledge, that
You thus have publish'd me ! Gentle my lord,
You scarce can right me thoroughly, then, to say
You did mistake.

Leo.   No ; if I mistake   100
In those foundations which I build upon,
The centre is not big enough to bear
A school-boy's top. Away with her, to prison!
He who shall speak for her is afar off guilty
But that he speaks.

Her.   There 's some ill planet reigns :
I must be patient till the heavens look
With an aspect more favourable. Good my lords,
I am not prone to weeping, as our sex
Commonly are ; the want of which vain dew
Perchance shall dry your pities : but I have   110

That honourable grief lodg'd here which burns
Worse than tears drown : beseech you all, my lords,
With thoughts so qualified, as your charities
Shall best instruct you, measure me ; and so
The king's will be perform'd !

Leo.   Shall I be heard ?

Her. Who is 't that goes with me ?   Beseech your highness,
My women may be with me, for you see
My plight requires it.   Do not weep, good fools,
There is no cause : when you shall know your
          mistress
Has deserv'd prison, then abound in tears   120
As I come out : this action I now go on
Is for my better grace.   Adieu, my lord :
I never wish'd to see you sorry, now
I trust I shall.   My women, come ; you have leave.

Leo. Go, do our bidding ; hence !

                    Exit Queen, guarded ; with Ladies

1.L. Beseech your highness, call the queen again.

Ant. Be certain what you do, sir, lest your justice
Prove violence, in the which three great ones suffer,
Yourself, your queen, your son.

1.L.   For her, my lord,
I dare my life lay down, and will do 't, sir,   130
Please you to accept it, that the queen is spotless

31

I' the eyes of heaven, and to you; I mean,
In this, which you accuse her.

Ant.   If it prove
She's otherwise, I'll keep my stables where   †
I lodge my wife, I'll go in couples with her;
Than when I feel, and see her, no farther trust her;
For every inch of woman in the world,
Ay, every dram of woman's flesh is false,
If she be.

Leo.   Hold your peaces.

1.L.   Good my lord,—

Ant. It is for you we speak, not for ourselves: 140
You are abus'd, and by some putter-on
That will be damn'd for 't; would I knew the villain,
I would land-damn him.   Be she honour-flaw'd,   †
I have three daughters; the eldest is eleven;
The second and the third, nine, and some five;
If this prove true, they 'll pay for 't: by mine honour,
I'll geld 'em all; fourteen they shall not see,
To bring false generations: they are co-heirs,
And I had rather glib myself than they
Should not produce fair issue.

Leo.   Cease, no more.   150
You smell this business with a sense as cold
As is a dead man's nose: but I do see 't, and feel 't,

As you feel doing thus ; and see withal   †
The instruments that feel.

Ant.   If it be so,
We need no grave to bury honesty :
There's not a grain of it, the face to sweeten
Of the whole dungy earth.

Leo.   What ? lack I credit ?

1.L. I had rather you did lack than I, my lord,
Upon this ground ; and more it would content me
To have her honour true than your suspicion,   160
Be blam'd for 't how you might.

Leo.   Why, what need we
Commune with you of this, but rather follow
Our forceful instigation ?   Our prerogative
Calls not your counsels, but our natural goodness
Imparts this ; which if you, or stupefied
Or seeming so, in skill, cannot, or will not
Relish a truth, like us, inform yourselves
We need no more of your advice : the matter
The loss, the gain, the ordering on't, is all
Properly ours.

Ant.   And I wish, my liege,   170
You had only in your silent judgement tried it,
Without more overture.

Leo.   How could that be ?

Either thou art most ignorant by age,
Or thou wert born a fool.   Camillo's flight,
Added to their familiarity,
(Which was as gross as ever touch'd conjecture,
That lack'd sight only, nought for approbation
But only seeing, all other circumstances
Made up to the deed,) doth push on this proceeding :
Yet, for a greater confirmation,   180
(For in an act of this importance 'twere
Most piteous to be wild) I have dispatch'd in post
To sacred Delphos, to Apollo's temple,
Cleomenes and Dion, whom you know
Of stuff'd sufficiency : now from the oracle
They will bring all, whose spiritual counsel had
Shall stop, or spur me.   Have I done well ?

1.L. Well done, my lord.

Leo. Though I am satisfied, and need no more
Than what I know, yet shall the oracle   190
Give rest to the minds of others ; such as he
Whose ignorant credulity will not
Come up to the truth.   So have we thought it good
From our free person she should be confin'd,
Lest that the treachery of the two, fled hence,
Be left her to perform.   Come, follow us,
We are to speak in public ; for this business

34

Will raise us all.

Ant. (*aside*)   To laughter, as I take it,
If the good truth were known.   *Exeunt*

SCENE II

A prison

Enter Paulina, a Gentleman, and Attendants

Pau. The keeper of the prison, call to him ;
Let him have knowledge who I am.   *Exit Gent.*
                                                              Good lady,
No court in Europe is too good for thee,
What dost thou then in prison ?
                          Re-enter Gentleman, with the Gaoler
                                                      Now, good sir,
You know me, do you not ?
Gao.   For a worthy lady
And one whom much I honour.
Pau.   Pray you, then,
Conduct me to the queen.
Gao.   I may not, madam :
To the contrary I have express commandment.
Pau. Here's ado,
To lock up honesty and honour from   10

The access of gentle visitors !   Is 't lawful, pray you,
To see her women ? any of them ? Emilia ?

Gao. So please you, madam,
To put apart these your attendants, I
Shall bring Emilia forth.

Pau.   I pray now, call her.
Withdraw yourselves.

> *Exeunt Gentleman and Attendants*

Gao.   And, madam,
I must be present at your conference.

Pau. Well, be 't so, prithee.   *Exit Gaoler*
Here 's such ado to make no stain a stain
As passes colouring.

> *Re-enter Gaoler, with Emilia*

                    Dear gentlewoman,
How fares our gracious lady ?   20

Em. As well as one so great, and so forlorn,
May hold together : on her frights and griefs,
(Which never tender lady hath borne greater)
She is, something before her time, deliver'd.

Pau. A boy ?

Em.   A daughter, and a goodly babe,
Lusty, and like to live : the queen receives
Much comfort in 't ; says ' My poor prisoner,
I am innocent as you.'

Pau.   I dare be sworn :
These dangerous unsafe lunes i' the king, beshrew
      them !   30
He must be told on 't, and he shall : the office
Becomes a woman best ; I 'll take 't upon me :
If I prove honey-mouth'd, let my tongue blister,
And never to my red-look'd anger be
The trumpet any more.   Pray you, Emilia,
Commend my best obedience to the queen :
If she dares trust me with her little babe,
I 'll show 't the king, and undertake to be
Her advocate to the loud'st.   We do not know
How he may soften at the sight o' the child :   40
The silence often of pure innocence
Persuades, when speaking fails.

Em.   Most worthy madam,
Your honour, and your goodness is so evident,
That your free undertaking cannot miss
A thriving issue : there is no lady living
So meet for this great errand ; please your ladyship
To visit the next room, I 'll presently
Acquaint the queen of your most noble offer,
Who but to-day hammer'd of this design,
But durst not tempt a minister of honour,   50
Lest she should be denied.

37

Pau.   Tell her, Emilia,
    I 'll use that tongue I have : if wit flow from 't
    As boldness from my bosom, let 't not be doubted
    I shall do good.

Em.   Now be you blest for it !
    I 'll to the queen : please you, come something nearer.

Gao. Madam, if 't please the queen to send the babe,
    I know not what I shall incur, to pass it,
    Having no warrant.

Pau.   You need not fear it, sir :
    This child was prisoner to the womb, and is
    By law and process of great nature thence   60
    Freed and enfranchis'd, not a party to
    The anger of the king, nor guilty of,
    (If any be) the trespass of the queen.

Gao. I do believe it.

Pau. Do not you fear : upon mine honour, I
    Will stand betwixt you and danger.   *Exeunt*

SCENE III

A room in Leontes' palace

Enter Leontes, Antigonus, Lords, and Servants

Leo. Nor night nor day no rest : it is but weakness
    To bear the matter thus ; mere weakness.   If

The cause were not in being,—part o' the cause,
She the adulteress ; for the harlot king
Is quite beyond mine arm, out of the blank
And level of my brain, plot-proof ; but she
I can hook to me : say that she were gone,
Given to the fire, a moiety of my rest
Might come to me again.   Who 's there ?

1.S. My lord !

Leo.   How does the boy ?

1.S.   He took good rest   10
To-night ; 'tis hop'd his sickness is discharg'd.

Leo. To see his nobleness !
Conceiving the dishonour of his mother,
He straight declin'd, droop'd, took it deeply,
Fasten'd and fix'd the shame on 't in himself ;
Threw off his spirit, his appetite, his sleep,
And downright languish'd.   Leave me solely : go,
See how he fares.   (*exit Serv.*)   Fie, fie ! no thought
    of him :
The very thought of my revenges that way
Recoil upon me : in himself too mighty,   20
And in his parties, his alliance ; let him be
Until a time may serve : for present vengeance,
Take it on her.   Camillo and Polixenes
Laugh at me ; make their pastime at my sorrow :

39

They should not laugh, if I could reach them, nor
Shall she, within my power.

Enter Paulina, with a child

1.*L.*   You must not enter.

Pau. Nay, rather, good my lords, be second to me:
Fear you his tyrannous passion more, alas,
Than the queen's life? a gracious innocent soul,
More free than he is jealous.

Ant.   That's enough.   30

2.*S.* Madam, he hath not slept to-night, commanded
None should come at him.

Pau.   Not so hot, good sir:
I come to bring him sleep. 'Tis such as you,
That creep like shadows by him, and do sigh
At each his needless heavings, such as you
Nourish the cause of his awaking: I
Do come with words as medicinal as true,
Honest as either, to purge him of that humour
That presses him from sleep.

Leo.   What noise there, ho?

Pau. No noise, my lord, but needful conference   40
About some gossips for your highness.

Leo.   How?
Away with that audacious lady! Antigonus,
I charg'd thee that she should not come about me.

I knew she would.

Ant.　　　　　　　I told her so, my lord,
On your displeasure's peril, and on mine,
She should not visit you.

Leo.　　　　　　　What? canst not rule her?

Pau. From all dishonesty he can: in this,
Unless he take the course that you have done,
Commit me for committing honour, trust it,
He shall not rule me.

Ant.　　　　　　La you now, you hear,　　　　　50
When she will take the rein, I let her run,
But she 'll not stumble.

Pau.　　　　　　　Good my liege, I come;
And, I beseech you, hear me, who professes
Myself your loyal servant, your physician,
Your most obedient counsellor; yet that dares
Less appear so, in comforting your evils,
Than such as most seem yours: I say, I come
From your good queen.

Leo.　　　　　　Good queen?

Pau.　　　　　　　Good queen, my lord,
Good queen; I say good queen;
And would by combat make her good, so were I　　60
A man, the worst about you.

Leo.　　　　　　Force her hence.

Pau. Let him that makes but trifles of his eyes
    First hand me : on mine own accord I 'll off,
    But first I 'll do my errand.   The good queen,
    (For she is good) hath brought you forth a daughter,
    Here 'tis ; commends it to your blessing.

                              Laying down the child

Leo.   Out !
    A mankind witch !   Hence with her, out o' door :
    A most intelligencing bawd !

Pau.   Not so :
    I am as ignorant in that as you
    In so entitling me ; and no less honest   70
    Than you are mad ; which is enough, I 'll warrant,
    (As this world goes) to pass for honest.

Leo.   Traitors !
    Will you not push her out ?   Give her the bastard.
    Thou dotard ! thou art woman-tir'd, unroosted
    By thy dame Partlet here.   Take up the bastard,
    Take 't up, I say ; give 't to thy crone.

Pau.   For ever
    Unvenerable be thy hands, if thou
    Tak'st up the princess by that forced baseness
    Which he has put upon 't !

Leo.   He dreads his wife.

Pau. So I would you did ; then 'twere past all doubt   80

You 'ld call your children, yours.

Leo.   A nest of traitors !

Ant. I am none, by this good light.

Pau.   Nor I ; nor any
But one that 's here ; and that 's himself ; for he
The sacred honour of himself, his queen's,
His hopeful son's, his babe's, betrays to slander,
Whose sting is sharper than the sword's ; and will not
(For, as the case now stands, it is a curse
He cannot be compell'd to 't) once remove
The root of his opinion, which is rotten
As ever oak or stone was sound.

Leo.   A callat   90
Of boundless tongue, who late hath beat her husband
And now baits me !   This brat is none of mine,
It is the issue of Polixenes :
Hence with it, and together with the dam
Commit them to the fire!

Pau.   It is yours ;
And, might we lay the old proverb to your charge,
So like you, 'tis the worse.   Behold, my lords,
Although the print be little, the whole matter
And copy of the father ; eye, nose, lip,
The trick of 's frown, his forehead, nay, the valley,   100
The pretty dimples of his chin and cheek ; his smiles ;

The very mould and frame of hand, nail, finger:
And thou, good goddess Nature, which hast made it
So like to him that got it, if thou hast
The ordering of the mind too, 'mongst all colours
No yellow in 't, lest she suspect, as he does,
Her children not her husband's!

Leo.   A gross hag!
And, lozel, thou art worthy to be hang'd,
That wilt not stay her tongue.

Ant.   Hang all the husbands
That cannot do that feat, you 'll leave yourself   110
Hardly one subject.

Leo.   Once more, take her hence.

Pau. A most unworthy and unnatural lord
Can do no more.

Leo.   I 'll ha' thee burnt.

Pau.   I care not:
It is an heretic that makes the fire,
Not she which burns in 't. I 'll not call you tyrant;
But this most cruel usage of your queen
(Not able to produce more accusation
Than your own weak-hing'd fancy) something savours
Of tyranny, and will ignoble make you,
Yea, scandalous to the world.

Leo.   On your allegiance,   120

Out of the chamber with her !   Were I a tyrant,
Where were her life ? she durst not call me so,
If she did know me one.   Away with her !

Pau. I pray you, do not push me, I 'll be gone.
Look to your babe, my lord, 'tis yours : Jove send her
A better guiding spirit !   What needs these hands ?
You, that are thus so tender o'er his follies,
Will never do him good, not one of you.
So, so : farewell, we are gone.   *Exit*

Leo. Thou, traitor, hast set on thy wife to this.   130
My child ? away with 't !   Even thou, that hast
A heart so tender o'er it, take it hence,
And see it instantly consum'd with fire ;
Even thou, and none but thou.   Take it up straight :
Within this hour bring me word 'tis done,
And by good testimony, or I 'll seize thy life,
With what thou else call'st thine : if thou refuse,
And wilt encounter with my wrath, say so ;
The bastard brains with these my proper hands
Shall I dash out.   Go, take it to the fire,   140
For thou set'st on thy wife.

Ant.   I did not, sir :
These lords, my noble fellows, if they please,
Can clear me in 't.

Lords.   We can ; my royal liege,

45

    He is not guilty of her coming hither.

Leo. You 're liars all.

1.L. Beseech your highness, give us better credit :
    We have always truly serv'd you, and beseech you
    So to esteem of us : and on our knees we beg,
    As recompense of our dear services
    Past and to come, that you do change this purpose,   150
    Which being so horrible, so bloody, must
    Lead on to some foul issue.   We all kneel.

Leo. I am a feather for each wind that blows :
    Shall I live on to see this bastard kneel
    And call me father ? better burn it now
    Than curse it then.   But be it ; let it live.
    It shall not neither.   You, sir, come you hither ;
    You that have been so tenderly officious
    With Lady Margery, your midwife there,   †
    To save this bastard's life,—for 'tis a bastard,   160
    So sure as this beard 's grey,—what will you adventure,
    To save this brat's life ?

Ant.   Any thing, my lord,
    That my ability may undergo,
    And nobleness impose : at least thus much ;
    I 'll pawn the little blood which I have left
    To save the innocent : any thing possible.

Leo. It shall be possible.   Swear by this sword

Thou wilt perform my bidding.

Ant.   I will, my lord.

Leo. Mark and perform it : seest thou ? for the fail

Of any point in 't shall not only be   170

Death to thyself, but to thy lewd-tongu'd wife,

(Whom for this time we pardon.)   We enjoin thee,

As thou art liege-man to us, that thou carry

This female bastard hence, and that thou bear it

To some remote and desert place, quite out

Of our dominions ; and that there thou leave it,

Without more mercy, to its own protection

And favour of the climate.   As by strange fortune

It came to us, I do in justice charge thee,

On thy soul's peril, and thy body's torture,   180

That thou commend it strangely to some place

Where chance may nurse or end it : take it up.

Ant. I swear to do this ; though a present death

Had been more merciful.   Come on, poor babe :

Some powerful spirit instruct the kites and ravens

To be thy nurses !   Wolves and bears, they say,

Casting their savageness aside, have done

Like offices of pity.   Sir, be prosperous

In more than this deed does require !   And blessing

Against this cruelty fight on thy side,   190

Poor thing, condemn'd to loss !   *Exit with the child*

47

Leo.   No, I 'll not rear
Another's issue.

Enter a Servant

Ser.   Please your highness, posts
From those you sent to the oracle are come
An hour since : Cleomenes and Dion,
Being well arriv'd from Delphos, are both landed,
Hasting to the court.

1.L.   So please you, sir, their speed
Hath been beyond account.

Leo.   Twenty three days
They have been absent : 'tis good speed ; foretells
The great Apollo suddenly will have
The truth of this appear.   Prepare you, lords,   200
Summon a session, that we may arraign
Our most disloyal lady ; for, as she hath
Been publicly accus'd, so shall she have
A just and open trial.   While she lives
My heart will be a burthen to me.   Leave me,
And think upon my bidding.   *Exeunt*

Act Third

SCENE I

Before a roadside inn in Sicilia †

Enter Cleomenes and Dion

Cle. The climate's delicate, the air most sweet,
Fertile the isle, the temple much surpassing †
The common praise it bears.

Dio.   I shall report,
For most it caught me, the celestial habits
(Methinks I so should term them) and the reverence
Of the grave wearers.   O, the sacrifice !
How ceremonious, solemn, and unearthly
It was i' the offering !

Cle.   But of all, the burst
And the ear-deafening voice o' the oracle,
Kin to Jove's thunder, so surpris'd my sense,   10
That I was nothing.

Dio.   If the event o' the journey
Prove as successful to the queen (O be 't so !)
As it hath been to us rare, pleasant, speedy,
The time is worth the use on 't.

Cle.   Great Apollo
     Turn all to the best !   These proclamations,
     So forcing faults upon Hermione,
     I little like.
Dio.   The violent carriage of it
     Will clear or end the business : when the oracle,
     Thus by Apollo's great divine seal'd up,
     Shall the contents discover, something rare   20
     Even then will rush to knowledge.   Go : fresh horses !
     And gracious be the issue.   *Exeunt*

SCENE II

A court of Justice

Enter Leontes, Lords, and Officers

Leo. This sessions (to our great grief we pronounce)
     Even pushes 'gainst our heart : the party tried,
     The daughter of a king, our wife, and one
     Of us too much belov'd.   Let us be clear'd
     Of being tyrannous, since we so openly
     Proceed in justice, which shall have due course,
     Even to the guilt, or the purgation.
     Produce the prisoner.
Off. It is his highness' pleasure, that the queen

Appear in person, here in court.   Silence!   10
   Enter Hermione guarded ; Paulina and Ladies attending

Leo. Read the indictment.

Off. (*reads*) Hermione, queen to the worthy Leontes, king
of Sicilia, thou art here accused and arraigned of high
treason, in committing adultery with Polixenes, king
of Bohemia, and conspiring with Camillo to take
away the life of our sovereign lord the king, thy
royal husband : the pretence whereof being by
circumstances partly laid open, thou, Hermione, contrary to the faith and allegiance of a true subject,
didst counsel and aid them, for their better safety,   20
to fly away by night.

Her. Since what I am to say must be but that
   Which contradicts my accusation, and
   The testimony on my part no other
   But what comes from myself, it shall scarce boot me
   To say ' not guilty : ' mine integrity,
   Being counted falsehood, shall, as I express it,
   Be so receiv'd.   But thus, if powers divine
   Behold our human actions (as they do)
   I doubt not then but innocence shall make   30
   False accusation blush, and tyranny
   Tremble at patience.   You, my lord, best know
   (Who least will seem to do so) my past life

Hath been as continent, as chaste, as true,
As I am now unhappy ; which is more
Than history can pattern, though devis'd
And play'd to take spectators.   For behold me,
A fellow of the royal bed, which owe
A moiety of the throne, a great king's daughter,
The mother to a hopeful prince, here standing   40
To prate and talk for life, and honour, 'fore
Who please to come and hear.   For life, I prize it
As I weigh grief, which I would spare : for honour,
'Tis a derivative from me to mine,
And only that I stand for.   I appeal
To your own conscience, sir, before Polixenes
Came to your court, how I was in your grace,
How merited to be so ; since he came,
With what encounter so uncurrent I   †
Have strain'd to appear thus ; if one jot beyond   50
The bound of honour, or in act, or will,
That way inclining, harden'd be the hearts
Of all that hear me, and my near'st of kin
Cry fie upon my grave !

Leo.   I ne'er heard yet
That any of these bolder vices wanted
Less impudence to gainsay what they did
Than to perform it first.

Her.   That's true enough ;
    Though 'tis a saying, sir, not due to me.

Leo. You will not own it.

Her.   More than mistress of   †
    Which comes to me in name of fault, I must not   60
    At all acknowledge.   For Polixenes
    (With whom I am accus'd) I do confess
    I lov'd him as in honour he requir'd,
    With such a kind of love as might become
    A lady like me ; with a love even such,
    So and no other, as yourself commanded :
    Which not to have done I think had been in me
    Both disobedience and ingratitude
    To you, and toward your friend, whose love had
        spoke,
    Even since it could speak, from an infant, freely   70
    That it was yours.   Now for conspiracy,
    I know not how it tastes, though it be dish'd
    For me to try how : all I know of it
    Is that Camillo was an honest man ;
    And why he left your court, the gods themselves
    (Wotting no more than I) are ignorant.

Leo. You knew of his departure, as you know
    What you have underta'en to do in 's absence.

Her. Sir,

You speak a language that I understand not: 80
My life stands in the level of your dreams,
Which I 'll lay down.

Leo.   Your actions are my dreams ;
You had a bastard by Polixenes,
And I but dream'd it.   As you were past all shame,
(Those of your fact are so) so past all truth :
Which to deny concerns more than avails ; for as
Thy brat hath been cast out, like to itself,
No father owning it (which is, indeed,
More criminal in thee than it) so thou
Shalt feel our justice in whose easiest passage   90
Look for no less than death.

Her.   Sir, spare your threats :
The bug which you would fright me with I seek.
To me can life be no commodity ;
The crown and comfort of my life, your favour,
I do give lost, for I do feel it gone,
But know not how it went.   My second joy,
And first-fruits of my body, from his presence
I am barr'd, like one infectious.   My third comfort,
Starr'd most unluckily, is from my breast,
The innocent milk in its most innocent mouth,   100
Hal'd out to murder : myself on every post
Proclaim'd a strumpet : with immodest hatred

The child-bed privilege denied, which 'longs
To women of all fashion ; lastly, hurried
Here to this place, i' the open air, before
I have got strength of limit.   Now, my liege,
Tell me what blessings I have here alive,
That I should fear to die ?   Therefore proceed.
But yet hear this ; mistake me not ; no life,
(I prize it not a straw) but for mine honour,   110
Which I would free, if I shall be condemn'd
Upon surmises (all proofs sleeping else
But what your jealousies awake) I tell you
'Tis rigour, and not law.   Your honours all,
I do refer me to the oracle :
Apollo be my judge !

1.L.   This your request
Is altogether just : therefore bring forth,
And in Apollo's name, his oracle.

        Exeunt certain Officers

Her. The Emperor of Russia was my father :
O that he were alive, and here beholding   120
His daughter's trial ! that he did but see
The flatness of my misery, yet with eyes
Of pity, not revenge !

   Re-enter Officers, with Cleomenes and Dion

Off. You here shall swear upon this sword of justice,

That you, Cleomenes and Dion, have
Been both at Delphos, and from thence have brought
This seal'd-up oracle, by the hand deliver'd
Of great Apollo's priest ; and that since then
You have not dar'd to break the holy seal
Nor read the secrets in 't.

Cle. Dio.   All this we swear.   130

Leo. Break up the seals and read.

Off. (*reads*) Hermione is chaste, Polixenes blameless,
Camillo a true subject, Leontes a jealous tyrant, his
innocent babe truly begotten, and the king shall live
without an heir, if that which is lost be not found.

Lords. Now blessed be the great Apollo !

Her.   Prais'd !

Leo. Hast thou read truth ?

Off.   Ay, my lord, even so
As it is here set down.

Leo. There is no truth at all i' the oracle :
The sessions shall proceed : this is mere falsehood.   140

Enter Servant

Ser. My lord the king, the king !

Leo.   What is the business ?

Ser. O sir, I shall be hated to report it !
The prince your son, with mere conceit, and fear
Of the queen's speed, is gone.

Leo.   How? gone?

Ser.   Is dead.

Leo. Apollo's angry, and the heavens themselves
Do strike at my injustice. (*Hermione faints.*) How
        now there?

Pau. This news is mortal to the queen: look down
And see what death is doing.

Leo.   Take her hence:
Her heart is but o'ercharg'd; she will recover:
I have too much believ'd mine own suspicion: 150
Beseech you, tenderly apply to her
Some remedies for life.

            Exeunt Paulina and Ladies, with Hermione
                Apollo, pardon
My great profaneness 'gainst thine oracle!
I'll reconcile me to Polixenes,
New woo my queen, recall the good Camillo,
Whom I proclaim a man of truth, of mercy;
For, being transported by my jealousies
To bloody thoughts, and to revenge, I chose
Camillo for the minister, to poison
My friend Polixenes: which had been done,   160
But that the good mind of Camillo tardied
My swift command, though I with death and with
Reward did threaten and encourage him,

Not doing it and being done : he, most humane
And fill'd with honour, to my kingly guest
Unclasp'd my practice, quit his fortunes here,
Which you knew great, and to the hazard
Of all incertainties himself commended,
No richer than his honour : how he glisters
Thorough my rust ! and how his piety   170
Does my deeds make the blacker !

Re-enter Paulina

Pau.   Woe the while !
    O, cut my lace, lest my heart, cracking it,
Break too !

1.L.   What fit is this ? good lady ?

Pau. What studied torments, tyrant, hast for me ?
What wheels ? racks ? fires ? what flaying ? boiling ?
In leads, or oils ? what old or newer torture
Must I receive, whose every word deserves
To taste of thy most worst ?   Thy tyranny
(Together working with thy jealousies,
Fancies too weak for boys, too green and idle   180
For girls of nine) O, think what they have done,
And then run mad indeed ; stark mad ! for all
Thy by-gone fooleries were but spices of it.
That thou betray'dst Polixenes, 'twas nothing ;
That did but show thee, of a fool, inconstant

And damnable ingrateful: nor was 't much,
Thou wouldst have poison'd good Camillo's honour,
To have him kill a king; poor trespasses,
More monstrous standing by: whereof I reckon
The casting forth to crows thy baby-daughter   190
To be or none or little; though a devil
Would have shed water out of fire ere done 't:
Nor is 't directly laid to thee, the death
Of the young prince, whose honourable thoughts
(Thoughts high for one so tender) cleft the heart
That could conceive a gross and foolish sire
Blemish'd his gracious dam: this is not, no,
Laid to thy answer: but the last,—O lords,
When I have said, cry 'woe!'—the queen, the queen,
The sweet'st, dear'st creature 's dead; and vengeance
    for 't   200
Not dropp'd down yet.

1.*L.*   The higher powers forbid!

Pau. I say she 's dead; I 'll swear 't. If word nor oath
Prevail not, go and see: if you can bring
Tincture or lustre in her lip, her eye,
Heat outwardly or breath within, I 'll serve you
As I would do the gods.   But, O thou tyrant!
Do not repent these things, for they are heavier
Than all thy woes can stir: therefore betake thee

To nothing but despair.　A thousand knees,
Ten thousand years together, naked, fasting, 21(
Upon a barren mountain, and still winter
In storm perpetual, could not move the gods
To look that way thou wert.

Leo.　　　　　　　　Go on, go on :
Thou canst not speak too much, I have deserv'd
All tongues to talk their bitterest.

1.L.　　　　　　　　Say no more ;
Howe'er the business goes, you have made fault
I' the boldness of your speech.

Pau.　　　　　　　I am sorry for 't :
All faults I make, when I shall come to know them,
I do repent.　Alas ! I have show'd too much
The rashness of a woman : he is touch'd 220
To the noble heart.　What's gone, and what's past
　help,
Should be past grief : do not receive affliction
At my petition ; I beseech you, rather
Let me be punish'd, that have minded you
Of what you should forget.　Now, good my liege,
Sir, royal sir, forgive a foolish woman :
The love I bore your queen, lo, fool again !
I 'll speak of her no more, nor of your children ;
I 'll not remember you of my own lord,

60

Who is lost too : take your patience to you,   230
And I 'll say nothing.

Leo.   Thou didst speak but well
When most the truth ; which I receive much better
Than to be pitied of thee.   Prithee bring me
To the dead bodies of my queen and son ;
One grave shall be for both ; upon them shall
The causes of their death appear, unto
Our shame perpetual.   Once a day I 'll visit
The chapel where they lie, and tears shed there
Shall be my recreation : so long as nature
Will bear up with this exercise, so long   240
I daily vow to use it.   Come, and lead me
To these sorrows.   *Exeunt*

SCENE III

Bohemia.   A desert country near the sea

Enter Antigonus with a Child, and a Mariner

Ant. Thou are perfect, then, our ship hath touch'd upon †
The deserts of Bohemia ?

Mar.   Ay, my lord, and fear
We have landed in ill time : the skies look grimly
And threaten present blusters.   In my conscience,

The heavens with that we have in hand are angry
And frown upon 's.

Ant. Their sacred wills be done ! Go, get aboard,
Look to thy bark, I 'll not be long before
I call upon thee.

Mar. Make your best haste, and go not   10
Too far i' the land : 'tis like to be loud weather ;
Besides, this place is famous for the creatures
Of prey that keep upon 't.

Ant.   Go thou away,
I 'll follow instantly.

Mar.   I am glad at heart
To be so rid o' the business.   *Exit*

Ant.   Come, poor babe :
I have heard (but not believ'd) the spirits o' the dead
May walk again : if such thing be, thy mother
Appear'd to me last night ; for ne'er was dream
So like a waking. To me comes a creature,
Sometimes her head on one side, some another ;   20
I never saw a vessel of like sorrow,
So fill'd, and so becoming : in pure white robes,
Like very sanctity, she did approach
My cabin where I lay ; thrice bow'd before me,
And, gasping to begin some speech, her eyes
Became two spouts : the fury spent, anon

Did this break from her : ' Good Antigonus,
Since fate, against thy better disposition,
Hath made thy person for the thrower-out
Of my poor babe, according to thine oath,   30
Places remote enough are in Bohemia,
There weep, and leave it crying ; and for the babe
Is counted lost for ever, Perdita
I prithee call 't.   For this ungentle business,
Put on thee by my lord, thou ne'er shalt see
Thy wife Paulina more.'   And so, with shrieks,
She melted into air.   Affrighted much,
I did in time collect myself, and thought
This was so, and no slumber.   Dreams are toys,
Yet for this once, yea, superstitiously,   40
I will be squar'd by this.   I do believe
Hermione hath suffer'd death, and that
Apollo would (this being indeed the issue
Of King Polixenes) it should here be laid,
Either for life or death, upon the earth
Of its right father.   Blossom, speed thee well !
There lie, and there thy character : there these,
Which may, if fortune please, both breed thee, pretty,
And still rest thine.   The storm begins, poor wretch,
That for thy mother's fault art thus expos'd   50
To loss, and what may follow !   Weep I cannot,

But my heart bleeds ; and most accurs'd am I
To be by oath enjoin'd to this.   Farewell !
The day frowns more and more : thou 'rt like to have
A lullaby too rough : I never saw
The heavens so dim, by day.   A savage clamour !
Well may I get aboard !   This is the chase :
I am gone for ever.   *Exit, pursued by a bear* †

Enter a Shepherd

She. I would there were no age between ten and three-
and-twenty, or that youth would sleep out the rest ;   6o
for there is nothing in the between but getting
wenches with child, wronging the ancientry, stealing,
fighting—Hark you now !   Would any but these
boil'd brains of nineteen and two-and-twenty hunt
this weather ?   They have scar'd away two of my
best sheep, which I fear the wolf will sooner find
than the master : if any where I have them, 'tis by
the sea-side, browzing of ivy.   Good luck (an 't be
thy will) what have we here ?   Mercy on 's, a
barne ?   very pretty barne !   A boy or a child, I   7o
wonder ?   A pretty one, a very pretty one : sure,
some scape : though I am not bookish, yet I can
read waiting-gentlewoman in the scape.   This has
been some stair-work, some trunk-work, some †
behind-door-work : they were warmer that got

64

this than the poor thing is here.   I'll take it up for pity, yet I'll tarry till my son come; he hallooed but even now.   Whoa, ho, hoa!

Enter Clown

Clo.   Hilloa, loa!

She.   What, art so near?   If thou'lt see a thing to talk on   80
when thou art dead and rotten, come hither.   What ail'st thou, man?

Clo.   I have seen two such sights, by sea and by land! but I am not to say it is a sea, for it is now the sky: betwixt the firmament and it you cannot thrust a bodkin's point.

She.   Why, boy, how is it?

Clo.   I would you did but see how it chafes, how it rages, how it takes up the shore; but that's not to the point.   O, the most piteous cry of the poor souls!   90
sometimes to see 'em, and not to see 'em; now the ship boring the moon with her main-mast, and anon swallowed with yest and froth, as you'ld thrust a cork into a hogshead.   And then for the land service, to see how the bear tore out his shoulder-bone, how he cried to me for help, and said his name was Antigonus, a nobleman.   But to make an end of the ship, to see how the sea flap-dragoned it: but, first, †
how the poor souls roar'd, and the sea mock'd

    them ; and how the poor gentleman roar'd and the 100
    bear mock'd him, both roaring louder than the sea
    or weather.

She. Name of mercy, when was this, boy ?

Clo. Now, now : I have not wink'd since I saw these
    sights : the men are not yet cold under water, nor
    the bear half din'd on the gentleman : he 's at it
    now.

She. Would I had been by, to have help'd the old man !

Clo. I would you had been by the ship side, to have
    help'd her : there your charity would have lack'd 110
    footing.

She. Heavy matters, heavy matters ! but look thee here,
    boy. Now bless thyself : thou met'st with things
    dying, I with things new-born. Here 's a sight for
    thee ; look thee, a bearing-cloth for a squire's
    child ! look thee here ; take up, take up, boy ;
    open 't. So, let 's see : it was told me I should
    be rich by the fairies. This is some changeling :
    open 't. What 's within, boy ?

Clo. You 're a made old man : if the sins of your youth 120
    are forgiven you, you 're well to live. Gold, all
    gold !

She. This is fairy gold, boy, and 'twill prove so : up
    with 't, keep it close : home, home, the next way.

We are lucky, boy, and to be so still requires nothing
but secrecy.   Let my sheep go : come, good boy,
the next way home.

Clo. Go you the next way with your findings, I'll go see
if the bear be gone from the gentleman, and how
much he hath eaten : they are never curst but when 130
they are hungry : if there be any of him left, I'll
bury it.

She. That's a good deed.   If thou mayest discern by
that which is left of him what he is, fetch me to the
sight of him.

Clo. Marry, will I ; and you shall help to put him i' the
ground.

She. 'Tis a lucky day, boy, and we'll do good deeds
on 't.   *Exeunt*

Act Fourth

SCENE I

Enter Time, the Chorus

*Time.*I, that please some, try all, both joy and terror
Of good and bad, that makes and unfolds error.
Now take upon me (in the name of Time)

To use my wings.   Impute it not a crime
To me, or my swift passage, that I slide
O'er sixteen years, and leave the growth untried
Of that wide gap, since it is in my power
To o'erthrow law, and in one self-born hour
To plant and o'erwhelm custom.   Let me pass
The same I am, ere ancient'st order was   10
Or what is now receiv'd : I witness to
The times that brought them in ; so shall I do
To the freshest things now reigning, and make stale
The glistering of this present, as my tale
Now seems to it.   Your patience this allowing,
I turn my glass, and give my scene such growing
As you had slept between : Leontes leaving
The effects of his fond jealousies, so grieving
That he shuts up himself ; imagine me,
Gentle spectators, that I now may be   20
In fair Bohemia, and remember well,
I mentioned a son o' the king's, which Florizel
I now name to you ; and with speed so pace
To speak of Perdita, now grown in grace
Equal with wondering : what of her ensues
I list not prophesy ; but let Time's news
Be known when 'tis brought forth.   A shepherd's
    daughter,

And what to her adheres, which follows after,
Is the argument of Time.   Of this allow,
If ever you have spent time worse ere now ;   30
If never, yet that Time himself doth say
He wishes earnestly you never may.   *Exit*

SCENE II

Bohemia.   The palace of Polixenes

Enter Polixenes and Camillo

Pol. I pray thee, good Camillo, be no more importunate :
'tis a sickness denying thee any thing ; a death **to**
grant this.

Cam. It is fifteen years since I saw my country : though
I have for the most part been aired abroad, I desire
to lay my bones there.   Besides, the penitent king,
my master, hath sent for me, to whose feeling
sorrows I might be some allay (or I o'erween to
think so) which is another spur to my departure.

Pol. As thou lov'st me, Camillo, wipe not out the rest   10
of thy services by leaving me now : the need I have
of thee, thine own goodness hath made ; better no**t**
to have had thee than thus to want thee : thou,
having made me businesses, which none without

69

thee can sufficiently manage, must either stay to execute them thyself, or take away with thee the very services thou hast done ; which if I have not enough considered (as too much I cannot) to be more thankful to thee shall be my study ; and my profit therein, the heaping friendships. Of that fatal 20 country, Sicilia, prithee speak no more, whose very naming punishes me with the remembrance of that penitent (as thou callest him) and reconciled king, my brother, whose loss of his most precious queen and children are even now to be afresh lamented. Say to me, when saw'st thou the Prince Florizel, my son ? Kings are no less unhappy, their issue not being gracious, than they are in losing them when they have approved their virtues.

Cam. Sir, it is three days since I saw the prince. What his 30 happier affairs may be, are to me unknown : but I have missingly noted, he is of late much retired from court, and is less frequent to his princely exercises than formerly he hath appeared.

Pol. I have considered so much, Camillo, and with some care, so far, that I have eyes under my service which look upon his removedness ; from whom I have this intelligence, that he is seldom from the house of a most homely shepherd ; a man, they say, that from

very nothing, and beyond the imagination of his   40
neighbours, is grown into an unspeakable estate.

Cam. I have heard, sir, of such a man, who hath a daughter
of most rare note : the report of her is extended more
than can be thought to begin from such a cottage.

Pol. That's likewise part of my intelligence ; but, I fear,
the angle that plucks our son thither.   Thou shalt
accompany us to the place, where we will (not
appearing what we are) have some question with the
shepherd ; from whose simplicity I think it not
uneasy to get the cause of my son's resort thither.   50
Prithee be my present partner in this business, and
lay aside the thoughts of Sicilia.

Cam. I willingly obey your command.

Pol. My best Camillo !   We must disguise ourselves.

Exeunt

SCENE III

A road near the Shepherd's cottage

Enter Autolycus, singing

When daffodils begin to peer,
   With heigh ! the doxy over the dale,
Why then comes in the sweet o' the yeat,
   For the red blood reigns in the winter's pale.

71

The white sheet bleaching on the hedge,
  With hey! the sweet birds, O, how they sing!
Doth set my pugging tooth on edge; †
  For a quart of ale is a dish for a king.

The lark, that tirra-lyra chants,
  With heigh! with hey! the thrush and the jay, 10
Are summer songs for me and my aunts,
  While we lie tumbling in the hay.

I have serv'd Prince Florizel, and in my time wore
three-pile, but now I am out of service:

But shall I go mourn for that, my dear?
  The pale moon shines by night:
And when I wander here and there,
  I then do most go right.

If tinkers may have leave to live,
  And bear the sow-skin budget, 20
Then my account I well may give,
  And in the stocks avouch it.

My traffic is sheets; when the kite builds, look to †
lesser linen. My father nam'd me Autolycus, who
being, as I am, litter'd under Mercury, was likewise †

a snapper-up of unconsidered trifles. With die and
drab I purchas'd this caparison, and my revenue is
the silly cheat. Gallows and knock are too powerful
on the highway : beating and hanging are terrors to
me : for the life to come, I sleep out the thought of it. 30
A prize ! a prize !

Enter Clown

Clo. Let me see, every 'leven wether tods, every tod yields
pound and odd shilling ; fifteen hundred shorn, what
comes the wool to ?

Aut. (*aside*) If the springe hold, the cock's mine.

Clo. I cannot do 't without counters. Let me see, what
am I to buy for our sheep-shearing feast ? Three
pound of sugar, five pound of currants, rice—what
will this sister of mine do with rice ? But my father
hath made her mistress of the feast, and she lays it on. 40
She hath made me four and twenty nosegays for the
shearers, three-man song-men all, and very good
ones ; but they are most of them means and bases ;
but one puritan amongst them, and he sings psalms
to hornpipes. I must have saffron to colour the
warden pies ; mace ; dates, none, that 's out of my
note ; nutmegs, seven ; a race or two of ginger, but
that I may beg ; four pound of prunes, and as many
of raisins o' the sun.

Aut. O that ever I was born !   *Grovelling on the ground* 50
†
Clo. I' the name of me !

Aut. O, help me, help me ! pluck but off these rags ; and
then, death, death !

Clo. Alack, poor soul, thou hast need of more rags to lay
on thee, rather than have these off.

Aut. O sir, the loathsomeness of them offends me more
than the stripes I have received, which are mighty
ones and millions.

Clo. Alas, poor man, a million of beating may come to a
great matter.   60

Aut. I am robb'd, sir, and beaten ; my money and apparel
ta'en from me, and these detestable things put upon
me.

Clo. What, by a horseman, or a footman ?

Aut. A footman, sweet sir, a footman.

Clo. Indeed, he should be a footman, by the garments he
has left with thee : if this be a horseman's coat, it
hath seen very hot service.   Lend me thy hand, I 'll
help thee : come, lend me thy hand.   *Helping him up*

Aut. O, good sir, tenderly, O !   70

Clo. Alas, poor soul !

Aut. O, good sir, softly, good sir ! I fear, sir, my
shoulder-blade is out.

Clo. How now ! canst stand ?

Aut. Softly, dear sir (*picks his pocket*); good sir, softly.
 You ha' done me a charitable office.

Clo. Dost lack any money? I have a little money for
 thee.

Aut. No, good sweet sir; no, I beseech you, sir: I have
 a kinsman not past three quarters of a mile hence, 80
 unto whom I was going; I shall there have money,
 or any thing I want: offer me no money, I pray you,
 that kills my heart.

Clo. What manner of fellow was he that robb'd you?

Aut. A fellow, sir, that I have known to go about with
 troll-my-dames: I knew him once a servant of the
 prince: I cannot tell, good sir, for which of his
 virtues it was, but he was certainly whipp'd out of
 the court.

Clo. His vices, you would say; there's no virtue whipp'd 90
 out of the court: they cherish it to make it stay
 there; and yet it will no more but abide.

Aut. Vices I would say, sir. I know this man well: he
 hath been since an ape-bearer, then a process-server,
 a bailiff, then he compass'd a motion of the Prodigal
 Son, and married a tinker's wife, within a mile
 where my land and living lies; and, having flown
 over many knavish professions, he settled only in
 rogue: some call him Autolycus.

Clo. Out upon him! prig, for my life, prig: he haunts 100
    wakes, fairs, and bear-baitings.

Aut. Very true, sir; he, sir, he; that's the rogue that put
    me into this apparel.

Clo. Not a more cowardly rogue in all Bohemia: if you
    had but look'd big and spit at him, he 'ld have
    run.

Aut. I must confess to you, sir, I am no fighter: I am
    false of heart that way, and that he knew, I warrant
    him.

Clo. How do you now? 110

Aut. Sweet sir, much better than I was; I can stand and
    walk: I will even take my leave of you, and pace
    softly towards my kinsman's.

Clo. Shall I bring thee on the way?

Aut. No, good-fac'd sir; no, sweet sir.

Clo. Then fare thee well: I must go buy spices for our
    sheep-shearing.

Aut. Prosper you, sweet sir! (*exit Clown.*) Your purse
    is not hot enough to purchase your spice. I'll be
    with you at your sheep-shearing too: if I make 120
    not this cheat bring out another, and the shearers
    prove sheep, let me be unroll'd and my name put
    in the book of virtue!

SONG

Jog on, jog on, the foot-path way,
And merrily hent the stile-a :
A merry heart goes all the day,
Your sad tires in a mile-a.   *Exit*

SCENE IV

The Shepherd's cottage

Enter Florizel and Perdita

Flo. These your unusual weeds to each part of you
Do give a life : no shepherdess, but Flora
Peering in April's front.   This your sheep-shearing
Is as a meeting of the petty gods,
And you the queen on 't.

Per.   Sir, my gracious lord,
To chide at your extremes it not becomes me :
(O, pardon, that I name them !)   Your high self,
The gracious mark o' the land, you have obscur'd
With a swain's wearing ; and me (poor lowly maid)   †
Most goddess-like prank'd up : but that our feasts   10
In every mess have folly, and the feeders
Digest it with a custom, I should blush
To see you so attir'd, sworn, I think,   †

77

To show myself a glass.

Flo.   I bless the time
When my good falcon made her flight across
Thy father's ground.

Per.   Now Jove afford you cause !
To me the difference forges dread ; (your greatness
Hath not been used to fear.)   Even now I tremble
To think your father, by some accident,
Should pass this way, as you did :   O, the Fates !   20
How would he look, to see his work, so noble,
Vilely bound up ?   What would he say ?   Or how
Should I (in these my borrow'd flaunts) behold
The sternness of his presence ?

Flo.   Apprehend
Nothing but jollity.   The gods themselves,
Humbling their deities to love, have taken
The shapes of beasts upon them :   Jupiter
Became a bull, and bellow'd ; the green Neptune
A ram, and bleated ; and the fire-rob'd god,
Golden Apollo, a poor humble swain,   30
As I seem now.   Their transformations
Were never for a piece of beauty rarer,
Nor in a way so chaste ; since my desires
Run not before mine honour, nor my lusts
Burn hotter than my faith.

Per.   O, but, sir,
  Your resolution cannot hold, when 'tis
  Oppos'd (as it must be) by the power of the king :
  One of these two must be necessities,
  Which then will speak, that you must change this
        purpose,
  Or I my life.

Flo.   Thou dearest Perdita,   40
  With these forc'd thoughts I prithee darken not
  The mirth o' the feast.   Or I 'll be thine, my fair,
  Or not my father's.   For I cannot be
  Mine own, nor any thing to any, if
  I be not thine.   To this I am most constant,
  Though destiny say no.   Be merry, gentle ;
  Strangle such thoughts as these with any thing
  That you behold the while.   Your guests are
        coming :
  Lift up your countenance, as it were the day
  Of celebration of that nuptial, which   50
  We two have sworn shall come.

Per.   O lady Fortune,
  Stand you auspicious !

Flo.   See, your guests approach :
  Address yourself to entertain them sprightly,
  And let 's be red with mirth.

Enter Shepherd, Clown, Mopsa, Dorcas, and others,
with Polixenes and Camillo disguised

She. Fie, daughter! when my old wife liv'd, upon
This day she was both pantler, butler, cook,
Both dame and servant; welcom'd all, serv'd all,
Would sing her song, and dance her turn: now here,
At upper end o' the table, now i' the middle;
On his shoulder, and his; her face o' fire   60
With labour, and the thing she took to quench it,
She would to each one sip. You are retir'd,
As if you were a feasted one, and not
The hostess of the meeting: pray you, bid
These unknown friends to 's welcome, for it is
A way to make us better friends, more known.
Come, quench your blushes, and present yourself
That which you are, mistress o' the feast: come on,
And bid us welcome to your sheep-shearing,
As your good flock shall prosper.

Per.   (*to Pol.*) Sir, welcome: 70
It is my father's will I should take on me
The hostess-ship o' the day. (*to Cam.*) You 're
    welcome, sir.
Give me those flowers there, Dorcas. Reverend sirs,
For you there 's rosemary and rue; these keep
Seeming and savour all the winter long:

80

Grace and remembrance be to you both,
And welcome to our shearing !

Pol.   Shepherdess,
(A fair one are you) well you fit our ages
With flowers of winter.

Per.   Sir, the year growing ancient, †
Not yet on summer's death, nor on the birth   80
Of trembling winter, the fairest flowers o' the season
Are our carnations and streak'd gillyvors,
Which some call nature's bastards : of that kind
Our rustic garden 's barren ; and I care not
To get slips of them.

Pol.   Wherefore, gentle maiden,
Do you neglect them ?

Per.   For I have heard it said
There is an art which in their piedness shares
With great creating nature.

Pol.   Say there be ;
Yet nature is made better by no mean,
But nature makes that mean : so, over that art   90
Which you say adds to nature, is an art
That nature makes.   You see, sweet maid, we marry
A gentler scion to the wildest stock,
And make conceive a bark of baser kind
By bud of nobler race : this is an art

Which does mend nature, change it rather, but
The art itself is nature.

Per.   So it is.

Pol. Then make your garden rich in gillyvors,
And do not call them bastards.

Per.   I'll not put
The dibble in earth to set one slip of them ;   100
No more than were I painted I would wish
This youth should say 'twere well, and only therefore
Desire to breed by me.   Here's flowers for you ;
Hot lavender, mints, savory, marjoram ;   †
The marigold, that goes to bed wi' the sun,
And with him rises, weeping : these are flowers
Of middle summer, and I think they are given
To men of middle age.   You're very welcome.

Cam. I should leave grazing, were I of your flock
And only live by gazing.

Per.   Out, alas !   110
You'ld be so lean, that blasts of January
Would blow you through and through.   Now, my
    fair'st friend,
I would I had some flowers o' the spring, that might
Become your time of day ; and yours, and yours,
That wear upon your virgin branches yet
Your maidenheads growing : O Proserpina,

For the flowers now, that (frighted) thou let'st fall
From Dis's waggon ! daffodils,
That come before the swallow dares, and take   †
The winds of March with beauty ; violets (dim,   120
But sweeter than the lids of Juno's eyes,
Or Cytherea's breath) ; pale primroses,
That die unmarried, ere they can behold
Bright Phœbus in his strength (a malady
Most incident to maids) ; bold oxlips, and
The crown imperial ; lilies of all kinds,
The flower-de-luce being one ! O, these I lack,
To make you garlands of ; and my sweet friend,
To strew him o'er and o'er !

Flo.   What, like a corse ?

Per. No, like a bank, for love to lie and play on ;   130
Not like a corse ; or if, not to be buried,
But quick, and in mine arms.   Come, take your
    flowers :
Methinks I play as I have seen them do
In Whitsun pastorals : sure this robe of mine
Does change my disposition.

Flo.   What you do
Still betters what is done.   When you speak, sweet,
I'ld have you do it ever : when you sing,
I'ld have you buy and sell so ; so give alms,

Pray so ; and, for the ordering your affairs,
To sing them too : when you do dance, I wish you   140
A wave o' the sea, that you might ever do
Nothing but that ; move still, still so,
And own no other function : each your doing,
(So singular, in each particular)
Crowns what you are doing in the present deeds,
That all your acts are queens.

Per.   O Doricles,
Your praises are too large : but that your youth,
And the true blood which peeps so fairly through 't,
Do plainly give you out an unstain'd shepherd,
With wisdom I might fear, my Doricles,   150
You woo'd me the false way.

Flo.   I think you have
As little skill to fear as I have purpose
To put you to 't.   But come, our dance, I pray :
Your hand, my Perdita : so turtles pair,
That never mean to part.

Per.   I 'll swear for 'em.

Pol. This is the prettiest low-born lass that ever
Ran on the green-sward : nothing she does or seems
But smacks of something greater than herself,
Too noble for this place.

Cam.   He tells her something

That makes her blood look out : good sooth, she is   160
The queen of curds and cream.

Clo.   Come on, strike up !

Dor. Mopsa must be your mistress : marry, garlic,
To mend her kissing with !

Mop.   Now, in good time !

Clo. Not a word, a word, we stand upon our manners.
Come, strike up !

    Music.   Here a dance of Shepherds and Shepherdesses

Pol. Pray you, good shepherd, what fair swain is this
Which dances with your daughter ?

She. They call him Doricles ; and boasts himself
To have a worthy feeding : but I have it
Upon his own report and I believe it ;   170
He looks like sooth.   He says he loves my daughter ;
I think so too ; for never gaz'd the moon
Upon the water, as he 'll stand and read
As 'twere my daughter's eyes : and, to be plain,
I think there is not half a kiss to choose
Who loves another best.

Pol.   She dances featly.

She. So she does any thing, though I report it,
That should be silent : if young Doricles
Do light upon her, she shall bring him that
Which he not dreams of.   180

Enter Servant

Ser. O master, if you did but hear the pedlar at the door,
you would never dance again after a tabor and pipe ;
no, the bagpipe could not move you : he sings
several tunes faster than you 'll tell money ; he utters
them as he had eaten ballads, and all men's ears grew
to his tunes.

Clo. He could never come better ; he shall come in. I
love a ballad but even too well, if it be doleful
matter merrily set down ; or a very pleasant thing
indeed and sung lamentably.   190

Ser. He hath songs for man, or woman, of all sizes ; no
milliner can so fit his customers with gloves : he has
the prettiest love-songs for maids, so without bawdry
(which is strange) ; with such delicate burthens of
dildos and fadings, ' jump her and thump her ; ' and †
where some stretch-mouth'd rascal would, as it were,
mean mischief and break a foul gap into the matter,
he makes the maid to answer ' Whoop, do me no
harm, good man ; ' puts him off, slights him, with
' Whoop, do me no harm, good man.'   200

Pol. This is a brave fellow.

Clo. Believe me, thou talkest of an admirable conceited
fellow.   Has he any unbraided wares ?

Ser. He hath ribbons of all the colours i' the rainbow ;

points, more than all the lawyers in Bohemia can
learnedly handle, though they come to him by the
gross : inkles, caddisses, cambrics, lawns : why, he
sings 'em over as they were gods or goddesses ; you
would think a smock were a she-angel, he so chants
to the sleeve-hand, and the work about the square   210
on 't.

Clo. Prithee bring him in, and let him approach singing.

Per. Forewarn him, that he use no scurrilous words in 's
tunes.   *Exit Servant*

Clo. You have of these pedlars, that have more in them
than you 'ld think, sister.

Per. Ay, good brother, or go about to think.

Enter Autolycus, singing

> Lawn as white as driven snow,
> Cypress black as e'er was crow,
> Gloves as sweet as damask roses,   220
> Masks for faces and for noses ;
> Bugle bracelet, necklace amber,
> Perfume for a lady's chamber ;
> Golden quoifs and stomachers,
> For my lads to give their dears ;
> Pins, and poking-sticks of steel,
> What maids lack from head to heel :

> Come buy of me, come; come buy, come buy;
> Buy, lads, or else your lasses cry
> Come buy.   230

Clo. If I were not in love with Mopsa, thou shouldst take no money of me, but being enthrall'd as I am, it will also be the bondage of certain ribbons and gloves.

Mop. I was promis'd them against the feast, but they come not too late now.

Dor. He hath promis'd you more than that, or there be liars.

Mop. He hath paid you all he promis'd you : may be, he has paid you more, which will shame you to give him again.   240

Clo. Is there no manners left among maids ? will they wear their plackets where they should bear their faces ? Is there not milking-time ? when you are going to bed ? or kiln-hole ? to whistle off these secrets, but you must be tittle-tattling before all our guests ? 'tis well they are whispering : clammer your † tongues, and not a word more.

Mop. I have done. Come, you promis'd me a tawdry-lace, † and a pair of sweet gloves.

Clo. Have I not told thee how I was cozen'd by the way, 250 and lost all my money ?

Aut. And indeed, sir, there are cozeners abroad, therefore
it behoves men to be wary.

Clo. Fear not thou, man, thou shalt lose nothing here.

Aut. I hope so, sir, for I have about me many parcels of
charge.

Clo. What hast here ? ballads ?

Mop. Pray now, buy some : I love a ballad in print o' life,
for then we are sure they are true.

Aut. Here 's one, to a very doleful tune, how a usurer's   260
wife was brought to bed of twenty money-bags at
a burthen, and how she long'd to eat adders' heads,
and toads carbonadoed.

Mop. Is it true, think you ?

Aut. Very true, and but a month old.

Dor. Bless me from marrying a usurer !

Aut. Here 's the midwife's name to 't, one Mistress Tale-
porter, and five or six honest wives that were present.
Why should I carry lies abroad ?

Mop. Pray you now, buy it.   270

Clo. Come on, lay it by : and let 's first see moe ballads ;
we 'll buy the other things anon.

Aut. Here 's another ballad of a fish, that appeared upon
the coast, on Wednesday the fourscore of April, forty
thousand fathom above water, and sung this ballad
against the hard hearts of maids : it was thought she

was a woman, and was turned into a cold fish for she
would not exchange flesh with one that lov'd her:
the ballad is very pitiful, and as true.

Dor. Is it true too, think you ?   280

Aut. Five justices' hands at it, and witnesses more than
my pack will hold.

Clo. Lay it by too : another.

Aut. This is a merry ballad, but a very pretty one.

Mop. Let 's have some merry ones.

Aut. Why, this is a passing merry one, and goes to the
tune of ' Two maids wooing a man : ' there 's scarce
a maid westward but she sings it ; 'tis in request, I
can tell you.

Mop. We can both sing it : if thou 'lt bear a part, thou   290
shalt hear ; 'tis in three parts.

Dor. We had the tune on 't, a month ago.

Aut. I can bear my part ; you must know 'tis my occupa-
tion: have at it with you.

SONG

A.   Get you hence, for I must go
Where it fits not you to know.

D. Whither ?   *M.* O, whither ?   *D.* Whither ?

M.   It becomes thy oath full well,
Thou to me thy secrets tell :

D. Me too ; let me go thither.   300

M. Or thou goest to the grange or mill :

D. If to either, thou dost ill.

    A. Neither.   *D.* What, neither ?   *A.* Neither.

D. Thou hast sworn my love to be ;

M. Thou hast sworn it more to me :

    Then whither goest ? say, whither ?

Clo. We 'll have this song out anon by ourselves : my
father and the gentlemen are in sad talk, and we 'll
not trouble them.   Come, bring away thy pack after
me.   Wenches, I 'll buy for you both.   Pedlar, let 's 310
have the first choice.   Follow me, girls.

                        Exit with Dorcas and Mopsa

Aut. And you shall pay well for 'em.   *Follows singing*

        Will you buy any tape,

        Or lace for your cape,

    My dainty duck, my dear-a ?

        Any silk, any thread,

        Any toys for your head,

    Of the new'st, and fin'st, fin'st wear-a ?

        Come to the pedlar ;

        Money 's a meddler,   320

    That doth utter all men's ware-a.   *Exit*

           Re-enter Servant

Ser. Master, there is three carters, three shepherds, three

neat-herds, three swine-herds, that have made themselves all men of hair, they call themselves Saltiers,
and they have a dance which the wenches say is a
gallimaufry of gambols, because they are not in 't;
but they themselves are o' the mind (if it be not too
rough for some that know little but bowling) it
will please plentifully.

She. Away! we 'll none on 't: here has been too much 330
homely foolery already. I know, sir, we weary you.

Pol. You weary those that refresh us: pray, let 's see
these four threes of herdsmen.

Ser. One three of them, by their own report, sir, hath
danc'd before the king; and not the worst of the
three but jumps twelve foot and a half by the squier.

She. Leave your prating: since these good men are
pleas'd, let them come in; but quickly now.

Ser. Why, they stay at door, sir. *Exit*

Here a dance of twelve Satyrs

Pol. O, father, you 'll know more of that hereafter. 340
   (*to Cam.*) Is it not too far gone? 'Tis time to part
   them.
   He 's simple, and tells much. How now, fair shepherd!
   Your heart is full of something that does take
   Your mind from feasting. Sooth, when I was young

And handed love as you do, I was wont
To load my she with knacks : I would have ransack'd
The pedlar's silken treasury, and have pour'd it
To her acceptance ; you have let him go,
And nothing marted with him.   If your lass
Interpretation should abuse, and call this   350
Your lack of love or bounty, you were straited
For a reply, at least if you make a care
Of happy holding her.

Flo.   Old sir, I know
She prizes not such trifles as these are :
The gifts she looks from me are pack'd and lock'd
Up in my heart ; which I have given already,
But not deliver'd.   O, hear me breathe my life
Before this ancient sir, who, it should seem,
Hath sometime lov'd !   I take thy hand, this hand,
As soft as dove's down and as white as it,   360
Or Ethiopian's tooth, or the fann'd snow, that 's bolted
By the northern blasts twice o'er.

Pol.   What follows this ?
How prettily the young swain seems to wash
The hand was fair before !   I have put you out :
But to your protestation ; let me hear
What you profess.

Flo.   Do, and be witness to 't.

93

Pol. And this my neighbour too?

Flo.   And he, and more
Than he, and men, the earth, the heavens, and all:
That, were I crown'd the most imperial monarch,
Thereof most worthy; were I the fairest youth   370
That ever made eye swerve, had force and knowledge
More than was ever man's, I would not prize them
Without her love; for her, employ them all,
Commend them, and condemn them to her service,
Or to their own perdition.

Pol.   Fairly offer'd.

Cam. This shows a sound affection.

She.   But, my daughter,
Say you the like to him?

Per.   I cannot speak
So well, nothing so well; no, nor mean better:
By the pattern of mine own thoughts I cut out
The purity of his.

She.   Take hands, a bargain!   380
And, friends unknown, you shall bear witness to 't:
I give my daughter to him, and will make
Her portion equal his.

Flo.   O, that must be
I' the virtue of your daughter: one being dead,
I shall have more than you can dream of yet;

94

Enough then for your wonder.   But, come on,
Contract us 'fore these witnesses.

She.   Come, your hand ;
And, daughter, yours.

Pol.   Soft, swain, awhile, beseech you,
Have you a father ?

Flo.   I have : but what of him ?

Pol. Knows he of this ?

Flo.   He neither does, nor shall.   390

Pol. Methinks a father
Is at the nuptial of his son a guest
That best becomes the table.   Pray you once more,
Is not your father grown incapable
Of reasonable affairs ? is he not stupid
With age and altering rheums ? can he speak ? hear ?
Know man from man ? dispute his own estate ?
Lies he not bed-rid ? and again does nothing
But what he did being childish ?

Flo.   No, good sir ;
He has his health, and ampler strength indeed   400
Than most have of his age.

Pol.   By my white beard,
You offer him, if this be so, a wrong
Something unfilial : reason my son
Should choose himself a wife, but as good reason

          The father (all whose joy is nothing else
          But fair posterity) should hold some counsel
          In such a business.

Flo.   I yield all this ;
          But for some other reasons, my grave sir,
          Which 'tis not fit you know, I not acquaint
          My father of this business.

Pol.   Let him know 't.   410

Flo. He shall not.

Pol.   Prithee, let him.

Flo.   No, he must not.

She. Let him, my son : he shall not need to grieve
          At knowing of thy choice.

Flo.   Come, come, he must not.
          Mark our contract.

Pol.   Mark your divorce, young sir,
                                        Discovering himself

          Whom son I dare not call ; thou art too base
          To be acknowledg'd : thou a sceptre's heir,
          That thus affects a sheep-hook ?   Thou, old traitor,
          I am sorry that by hanging thee I can
          But shorten thy life one week.   And thou, fresh piece
          Of excellent witchcraft, who of force must know   420
          The royal fool thou cop'st with,—

She.   O, my heart !

                              96

Pol. I 'll have thy beauty scratch'd with briers, and made
More homely than thy state.   For thee, fond boy,
If I may ever know thou dost but sigh
That thou no more shalt see this knack (as never
I mean thou shalt) we 'll bar thee from succession,
Not hold thee of our blood, no, not our kin,
Farre than Deucalion off : mark thou my words :
Follow us to the court.   Thou churl, for this time,
Though full of our displeasure, yet we free thee   430
From the dead blow of it.   And you, enchantment,
Worthy enough a herdsman ; yea, him too,
That makes himself, but for our honour therein,
Unworthy thee,—if ever henceforth thou
These rural latches to his entrance open,
Or hoop his body more with thy embraces,
I will devise a death as cruel for thee
As thou art tender to 't.   *Exit*

Per.   Even here undone !   †
I was not much afeard ; for once or twice
I was about to speak, and tell him plainly,   440
The selfsame sun that shines upon his court
Hides not his visage from our cottage, but
Looks on alike.   Will 't please you, sir, be gone ?
I told you what would come of this : beseech you.
Of your own state take care : this dream of mine,—

²⁰ *h*   97

Being now awake, I 'll queen it no inch farther,
But milk my ewes, and weep.

Cam.   Why, how now, father;
Speak ere thou diest.

She.   I cannot speak, nor think,
Nor dare to know that which I know.   O sir!
You have undone a man of fourscore three,   450
That thought to fill his grave in quiet; yea,
To die upon the bed my father died,
To lie close by his honest bones: but now
Some hangman must put on my shroud, and lay me
Where no priest shovels in dust.   O cursed wretch,
That knew'st this was the prince, and wouldst
    adventure
To mingle faith with him!   Undone! undone!
If I might die within this hour, I have liv'd
To die when I desire.   *Exit*

Flo.   Why look you so upon me?
I am but sorry, not afeard; delay'd,   460
But nothing alter'd: what I was, I am;
More straining on for plucking back; not following
My leash unwillingly.

Cam.   Gracious my lord,
You know your father's temper: at this time
He will allow no speech (which I do guess

You do not purpose to him) ; and as hardly
Will he endure your sight as yet, I fear :
Then, till the fury of his highness settle,
Come not before him.

Flo.   I not purpose it.
I think, Camillo ?

Cam.   Even he, my lord.   470

Per. How often have I told you 'twould be thus !
How often said, my dignity would last
But till 'twere known ?

Flo.   It cannot fail, but by
The violation of my faith, and then
Let nature crush the sides o' the earth together
And mar the seeds within !   Lift up thy looks :
From my succession wipe me, father, I
Am heir to my affection.

Cam.   Be advis'd.

Flo. I am, and by my fancy : if my reason
Will thereto be obedient, I have reason ;   480
If not, my senses, better pleas'd with madness,
Do bid it welcome.

Cam.   This is desperate, sir.

Flo. So call it : but it does fulfil my vow ;
I needs must think it honesty.   Camillo,
Not for Bohemia, nor the pomp that may

99

    Be thereat glean'd ; for all the sun sees, or
    The close earth wombs, or the profound seas hide
    In unknown fathoms, will I break my oath
    To this my fair belov'd : therefore, I pray you,
    As you have ever been my father's honour'd friend,   490
    When he shall miss me (as, in faith, I mean not
    To see him any more), cast your good counsels
    Upon his passion : let myself and fortune
    Tug for the time to come.   This you may know
    And so deliver, I am put to sea
    With her whom here I cannot hold on shore ;
    And most opportune to our need I have
    A vessel rides fast by, but not prepar'd
    For this design.   What course I mean to hold
    Shall nothing benefit your knowledge, nor   500
    Concern me the reporting.

Cam.   O my lord !
    I would your spirit were easier for advice,
    Or stronger for your need.

Flo.   Hark, Perdita.   *Drawing her aside*
    I'll hear you by and by.

Cam.   He's irremoveable,
    Resolv'd for flight.   Now were I happy, if
    His going I could frame to serve my turn,
    Save him from danger, do him love and honour,

Purchase the sight again of dear Sicilia
And that unhappy king, my master, whom
I so much thirst to see.

Flo.   Now, good Camillo ;   510
I am so fraught with curious business that
I leave out ceremony.

Cam.   Sir, I think
You have heard of my poor services, i' the love
That I have borne your father ?

Flo.   Very nobly
Have you deserv'd : it is my father's music
To speak your deeds ; not little of his care
To have them recompens'd as thought on.

Cam.   Well, my lord,
If you may please to think I love the king,
And through him what is nearest to him, which is
Your gracious self, embrace but my direction,   520
If your more ponderous and settled project
May suffer alteration : on mine honour
I'll point you where you shall have such receiving
As shall become your highness, where you may
Enjoy your mistress, from the whom, I see,
There's no disjunction to be made, but by
(As heavens forefend !) your ruin ; marry her,
And, with my best endeavours in your absence,

Your discontenting father strive to qualify
And bring him up to liking.

Flo. How, Camillo, 530
May this, almost a miracle, be done?
That I may call thee something more than man
And after that trust to thee.

Cam. Have you thought on
A place whereto you'll go?

Flo. Not any yet:
But as the unthought-on accident is guilty
To what we wildly do, so we profess
Ourselves to be the slaves of chance, and flies
Of every wind that blows.

Cam. Then list to me:
This follows, if you will not change your purpose
But undergo this flight; make for Sicilia, 540
And there present yourself, and your fair princess,
(For so I see she must be) 'fore Leontes:
She shall be habited as it becomes
The partner of your bed. Methinks I see
Leontes opening his free arms, and weeping
His welcomes forth; asks thee the son forgiveness,
As 'twere i' the father's person; kisses the hands
Of your fresh princess; o'er and o'er divides him
'Twixt his unkindness and his kindness; the one

He chides to hell, and bids the other grow   550
Faster than thought, or time.

Flo.   Worthy Camillo,
What colour for my visitation shall I
Hold up before him ?

Cam.   Sent by the king your father
To greet him, and to give him comforts.   Sir,
The manner of your bearing towards him, with
What you (as from your father) shall deliver,
Things known betwixt us three, I 'll write you down,
The which shall point you forth at every sitting
What you must say ; that he shall not perceive
But that you have your father's bosom there   560
And speak his very heart.

Flo.   I am bound to you :
There is some sap in this.

Cam.   A course more promising
Than a wild dedication of yourselves
To unpath'd waters, undream'd shores ; most certain
To miseries enough : no hope to help you,
But as you shake off one to take another :
Nothing so certain as your anchors, who
Do their best office, if they can but stay you
Where you 'll be loath to be : besides you know
Prosperity 's the very bond of love,   570

Whose fresh complexion and whose heart together
Affliction alters.

Per.   One of these is true:
I think affliction may subdue the cheek,
But not take in the mind.

Cam.   Yea? say you so?
There shall not at your father's house these seven years
Be born another such.

Flo.   My good Camillo,
She is as forward of her breeding as
She is i' the rear o' our birth.

Cam.   I cannot say 'tis pity
She lacks instructions, for she seems a mistress
To most that teach.

Per.   Your pardon, sir; for this   580
I'll blush you thanks.

Flo.   My prettiest Perdita!
But O, the thorns we stand upon! Camillo,
Preserver of my father, now of me,
The medicine of our house, how shall we do?
We are not furnish'd like Bohemia's son,
Nor shall appear in Sicilia.

Cam.   My lord,
Fear none of this: I think you know my fortunes
Do all lie there: it shall be so my care

To have you royally appointed as if
The scene you play were mine.   For instance, sir,   590
That you may know you shall not want, one word.

They talk aside

Re-enter Autolycus

Aut. Ha, ha ! what a fool Honesty is ! and Trust, his
sworn brother, a very simple gentleman ! I have
sold all my trumpery ; not a counterfeit stone, not a
ribbon, glass, pomander, brooch, table-book, ballad,
knife, tape, glove, shoe-tie, bracelet, horn-ring, to
keep my pack from fasting : they throng who
should buy first, as if my trinkets had been hallowed,
and brought a benediction to the buyer : by which
means I saw whose purse was best in picture ; and   600
what I saw, to my good use I remembered.   My
clown (who wants but something to be a reasonable
man) grew so in love with the wenches' song, that
he would not stir his pettitoes till he had both tune
and words, which so drew the rest of the herd to me,
that all their other senses stuck in ears : you might
have pinch'd a placket, it was senseless ; 'twas
nothing to geld a codpiece of a purse ; I would
have fil'd keys off that hung in chains : no hearing,
no feeling, but my sir's song, and admiring the   610
nothing of it.   So that in this time of lethargy I

pick'd and cut most of their festival purses; and
had not the old man come in with a whoo-bub
against his daughter and the king's son, and scar'd
my choughs from the chaff, I had not left a purse
alive in the whole army.

    Camillo, Florizel, and Perdita come forward

Cam. Nay, but my letters, by this means being there
 So soon as you arrive, shall clear that doubt.

Flo. And those that you 'll procure from King Leontes—

Cam. Shall satisfy your father.

Per.   Happy be you!   620
 All that you speak shows fair.

Cam.   Who have we here?

         Seeing Autolycus

 We 'll make an instrument of this; omit
 Nothing may give us aid.

Aut. If they have overheard me now, why, hanging.

Cam. How now, good fellow! why shak'st thou so?
 Fear not, man, here 's no harm intended to thee.

Aut. I am a poor fellow, sir.

Cam. Why, be so still; here 's nobody will steal that from
 thee: yet for the outside of thy poverty we must
 make an exchange; therefore discase thee instantly, 630
 —thou must think there 's a necessity in 't,—and
 change garments with this gentleman: though the

    pennyworth on his side be the worst, yet hold thee,
    there's some boot.

*Aut.*I am a poor fellow, sir.   (*aside*) I know ye well
    enough.

*Cam.*Nay, prithee, dispatch : the gentleman is half flayed
    already.

*Aut.*Are you in earnest, sir ?   (*aside*) I smell the trick
    on 't.   640

Flo. Dispatch, I prithee.

*Aut.*Indeed, I have had earnest, but I cannot with con-
    science take it.

*Cam.*Unbuckle, unbuckle.

              Florizel and Autolycus exchange garments

    Fortunate mistress (let my prophecy
    Come home to ye !) you must retire yourself
    Into some covert : take your sweetheart's hat
    And pluck it o'er your brows, muffle your face,
    Dismantle you, and, as you can, disliken
    The truth of your own seeming, that you may,   650
    (For I do fear eyes over) to shipboard
    Get undescried.

Per.   I see the play so lies
    That I must bear a part.

Cam.   No remedy.
    Have you done there ?

Flo.   Should I now meet my father,
     He would not call me son.

Cam.   Nay, you shall have no hat.
                               Giving it to Perdita
     Come, lady, come.   Farewell, my friend.

Aut.   Adieu, sir.

Flo. O Perdita, what have we twain forgot !
     Pray you, a word.

Cam.(*aside*) What I do next, shall be to tell the king
     Of this escape, and whither they are bound ;   660
     Wherein my hope is I shall so prevail
     To force him after : in whose company
     I shall review Sicilia, for whose sight
     I have a woman's longing.

Flo.   Fortune speed us !
     Thus we set on, Camillo, to the sea-side.

Cam. The swifter speed the better.
                   Exeunt Florizel, Perdita, and Camillo

Aut. I understand the business, I hear it : to have an open
ear, a quick eye, and a nimble hand, is necessary for
a cut-purse ; a good nose is requisite also, to smell
out work for the other senses. I see this is the 670
time that the unjust man doth thrive. What an
exchange had this been without boot ! What a
boot is here with this exchange ! Sure the gods do

this year connive at us, and we may do any thing
extempore.   The prince himself is about a piece of
iniquity, stealing away from his father with his clog
at his heels : if I thought it were a piece of honesty
to acquaint the king withal, I would not do 't : I
hold it the more knavery to conceal it ; and therein
am I constant to my profession.   680

Re-enter Clown and Shepherd

Aside, aside, here is more matter for a hot brain :
every lane's end, every shop, church, session, hanging, yields a careful man work.

Clo. See, see ; what a man you are now ! There is no
other way but to tell the king she 's a changeling,
and none of your flesh and blood.

She. Nay, but hear me.

Clo. Nay, but hear me.

She. Go to, then.

Clo. She being none of your flesh and blood, your flesh 690
and blood has not offended the king, and so your
flesh and blood is not to be punish'd by him.   Show
those things you found about her (those secret things,
all but what she has with her) : this being done, let
the law go whistle : I warrant you.

She. I will tell the king all, every word, yea, and his son's

pranks too ; who, I may say, is no honest man,
neither to his father, nor to me, to go about to make
me the king's brother-in-law.

Clo. Indeed, brother-in-law was the farthest off you 700
could have been to him, and then your blood had
been the dearer by I know how much an ounce.

Aut.(aside) Very wisely, puppies !

She. Well, let us to the king : there is that in this fardel
will make him scratch his beard.

Aut.(aside) I know not what impediment this complaint
may be to the flight of my master.

Clo. Pray heartily he be at palace.

Aut.(aside) Though I am not naturally honest, I am so
sometimes by chance : let me pocket up my pedlar's 710
excrement. (*Takes off his false beard.*) How now,
rustics ! whither are you bound ?

She. To the palace, an it like your worship.

Aut. Your affairs there, what, with whom, the condition
of that fardel, the place of your dwelling, your
names, your ages, of what having, breeding, and
any thing that is fitting to be known, discover.

Clo. We are but plain fellows, sir.

Aut. A lie ; you are rough and hairy. Let me have no
lying : it becomes none but tradesmen, and they 720
often give us soldiers the lie : but we pay them for it

      with stamped coin, not stabbing steel ; therefore
      they do not give us the lie.

Clo. Your worship had like to have given us one, if you
      had not taken yourself with the manner.

She. Are you a courtier, an 't like you, sir ?

Aut. Whether it like me or no, I am a courtier.   Seest
      thou not the air of the court, in these enfoldings ?
      hath not my gait in it the measure of the court ?
      receives not thy nose court-odour from me ? reflect 730
      I not on thy baseness court-contempt ?   Thinkest
      thou, for that I insinuate, or toaze from thee thy
      business, I am therefore no courtier ?   I am courtier
      cap-a-pe ; and one that will either push on or pluck
      back thy business there : whereupon I command
      thee to open thy affair.

She. My business, sir, is to the king.

Aut. What advocate hast thou to him ?

She. I know not, an 't like you.

Clo. Advocate 's the court-word for a pheasant : say you †
      have none.   741

She. None, sir ; I have no pheasant, cock nor hen.

Aut. How bless'd are we that are not simple men !
      Yet nature might have made me as these are,
      Therefore I will not disdain.

Clo. This cannot be but a great courtier.

She. His garments are rich, but he wears them not handsomely.

Clo. He seems to be the more noble, in being fantastical : a great man, I'll warrant ; I know by the picking 750 on 's teeth.

Aut. The fardel there ? what 's i' the fardel ? Wherefore that box ?

She. Sir, there lies such secrets in this fardel and box, which none must know but the king, and which he shall know within this hour, if I may come to the speech of him.

Aut. Age, thou hast lost thy labour.

She. Why, sir ?

Aut. The king is not at the palace, he is gone aboard a new 760 ship to purge melancholy and air himself : for, if thou beest capable of things serious, thou must know the king is full of grief.

She. So 'tis said, sir ; about his son, that should have married a shepherd's daughter.

Aut. If that shepherd be not in hand-fast, let him fly : the curses he shall have, the tortures he shall feel, will break the back of man, the heart of monster.

Clo. Think you so, sir ?

Aut. Not he alone shall suffer what wit can make heavy, 770 and vengeance bitter ; but those that are germane to

him (though removed fifty times) shall all come
under the hangman : which, though it be great
pity, yet it is necessary. An old sheep-whistling
rogue, a ram-tender, to offer to have his daughter
come into grace ? Some say he shall be ston'd ;
but that death is too soft for him, say I : draw our
throne into a sheep-cote ? all deaths are too few,
the sharpest too easy.

Clo. Has the old man e'er a son, sir, do you hear, an 't 780
like you, sir ?

Aut. He has a son, who shall be flay'd alive, then 'nointed
over with honey, set on the head of a wasp's nest,
then stand till he be three-quarters and a dram dead ;
then recover'd again with aqua-vitæ or some other
hot infusion ; then, raw as he is, and in the hottest
day prognostication proclaims, shall he be set against
a brick-wall, the sun looking with a southward eye
upon him, where he is to behold him with flies
blown to death.   But what talk we of these traitorly 790
rascals, whose miseries are to be smil'd at, their
offences being so capital ?   Tell me (for you seem
to be honest plain men) what you have to the king :
being something gently consider'd, I 'll bring you
where he is aboard, tender your persons to his
presence, whisper him in your behalfs ; and if it be in

  man besides the king to effect your suits, here is man shall do it.

Clo. He seems to be of great authority : close with him, give him gold ; and though authority be a stubborn 800 bear, yet he is oft led by the nose with gold : show the inside of your purse to the outside of his hand, and no more ado. Remember ' ston'd,' and ' flay'd alive.'

She. An 't please you, sir, to undertake the business for us, here is that gold I have : I 'll make it as much more and leave this young man in pawn till I bring it you.

Aut. After I have done what I promis'd ?

She. Ay, sir.

Aut. Well, give me the moiety. Are you a party in this 810 business ?

Clo. In some sort, sir : but though my case be a pitiful one, I hope I shall not be flay'd out of it.

Aut. O, that 's the case of the shepherd's son : hang him, he 'll be made an example.

Clo. Comfort, good comfort ! We must to the king and show our strange sights : he must know 'tis none of your daughter, nor my sister ; we are gone else. Sir, I will give you as much as this old man does when the business is performed, and remain, as he 820 says, your pawn till it be brought you.

Aut. I will trust you.   Walk before toward the sea-side ;
go on the right hand : I will but look upon the
hedge and follow you.

Clo. We are blest in this man, as I may say, even blest.

She. Let's before, as he bids us : he was provided to do
us good.   *Exeunt Shepherd and Clown*

Aut. If I had a mind to be honest, I see Fortune would not
suffer me : she drops booties in my mouth.   I am
courted now with a double occasion ; gold, and a   830
means to do the prince my master good ; which who
knows how that may turn back to my advancement ?
I will bring these two moles, these blind ones, aboard
him : if he think it fit to shore them again, and that
the complaint they have to the king concerns him
nothing, let him call me rogue for being so far
officious ; for I am proof against that title, and
what shame else belongs to 't.   To him will I present
them, there may be matter in it.   *Exit*

Act Fifth

SCENE I

A room in Leontes' palace

Enter Leontes, Cleomenes, Dion, Paulina, and Servants

Cle. Sir, you have done enough, and have perform'd
A saint-like sorrow : no fault could you make,
Which you have not redeem'd ; indeed, paid down
More penitence than done trespass : at the last,
Do as the heavens have done ; forget your evil,
With them forgive yourself.

Leo.   Whilst I remember
Her, and her virtues, I cannot forget
My blemishes in them, and so still think of
The wrong I did myself : which was so much,
That heirless it hath made my kingdom, and   10
Destroy'd the sweet'st companion that e'er man
Bred his hopes out of ; true.

Pau.   Too true, my lord :
If, one by one, you wedded all the world,
Or from the all that are took something good,
To make a perfect woman, she you kill'd

Would be unparallel'd.

Leo.   I think so.   Kill'd?
She I kill'd?   I did so: but thou strikest me
Sorely, to say I did; it is as bitter
Upon thy tongue as in my thought: now, good now,
Say so but seldom.

Cle.   Not at all, good lady: 20
You might have spoken a thousand things that would
Have done the time more benefit, and grac'd
Your kindness better.

Pau.   You are one of those
Would have him wed again.

Dio.   If you would not so,
You pity not the state, nor the remembrance
Of his most sovereign name; consider little
What dangers, by his highness' fail of issue,
May drop upon his kingdom, and devour
Incertain lookers on.   What were more holy
Than to rejoice the former queen is well?   30
What holier than, for royalty's repair,
For present comfort, and for future good,
To bless the bed of majesty again
With a sweet fellow to't?

Pau.   There is none worthy,
Respecting her that's gone.   Besides, the gods

Will have fulfill'd their secret purposes;
For has not the divine Apollo said,
Is 't not the tenor of his oracle,
That King Leontes shall not have an heir
Till his lost child be found? which that it shall,   40
Is all as monstrous to our human reason
As my Antigonus to break his grave
And come again to me; who, on my life,
Did perish with the infant.   'Tis your counsel
My lord should to the heavens be contrary,
Oppose against their wills.   (*to Leontes*) Care not
          for issue;
The crown will find an heir: great Alexander
Left his to the worthiest; so his successor
Was like to be the best.

Leo.   Good Paulina,
Who hast the memory of Hermione,   50
I know, in honour, O, that ever I
Had squar'd me to thy counsel!—then, even now,
I might have look'd upon my queen's full eyes,
Have taken treasure from her lips.

Pau.   And left them
More rich for what they yielded.

Leo.   Thou speak'st truth.
No more such wives, therefore, no wife: one worse,

And better us'd, would make her sainted spirit
Again possess her corpse, and on this stage,
Where we offenders move, appear soul-vex'd,
And begin, ' Why to me ? '

Pau.   Had she such power,   60
She had just such cause.

Leo.   She had, and would incense me
To murder her I married.

Pau.   I should so.
Were I the ghost that walk'd, I 'ld bid you mark
Her eye, and tell me of what dull part in 't
You chose her ; then I 'ld shriek, that even your ears
Should rift to hear me, and the words that follow'd
Should be ' Remember mine.'

Leo.   Stars, stars,
And all eyes else, dead coals !   Fear thou no wife ;
I 'll have no wife, Paulina.

Pau.   Will you swear
Never to marry, but by my free leave ?   70

Leo. Never, Paulina ; so be bless'd my spirit !

Pau. Then, good my lords, bear witness to his oath.

Cle. You tempt him over-much.

Pau.   Unless another,
As like Hermione as is her picture,
Affront his eye.

Cle.   Good madam, I have done.

Pau. Yet, if my lord will marry,—if you will, sir,
    No remedy, but you will,—give me the office
    To choose you a queen : she shall not be so young
    As was your former, but she shall be such
    As (walk'd your first queen's ghost) it should take   80
       joy
    To see her in your arms.

Leo.   My true Paulina,
    We shall not marry till thou bid'st us.

Pau.   That
    Shall be when your first queen's again in breath ;
    Never till then.

              Enter a Gentleman

Gen. One that gives out himself Prince Florizel,
    Son of Polixenes, with his princess (she
    The fairest I have yet beheld) desires access
    To your high presence.

Leo.   What with him ? he comes not
    Like to his father's greatness : his approach,
    So out of circumstance and sudden, tells us   90
    'Tis not a visitation fram'd, but forc'd
    By need and accident.   What train ?

Gen.   But few,
    And those but mean.

Leo.   His princess, say you, with him ?

Gen. Ay, the most peerless piece of earth, I think,
  That e'er the sun shone bright on.

Pau.   O Hermione,
  As every present time doth boast itself
  Above a better gone, so must thy grave
  Give way to what's seen now !   Sir, you yourself
  Have said and writ so, but your writing now
  Is colder than that theme, ' She had not been,   100
  Nor was not to be equall'd ; '—thus your verse
  Flow'd with her beauty once : 'tis shrewdly ebb'd,
  To say you have seen a better.

Gen.   Pardon, madam :
  The one I have almost forgot (your pardon),
  The other, when she has obtain'd your eye,
  Will have your tongue too.   This is a creature,
  Would she begin a sect, might quench the zeal
  Of all professors else ; make proselytes
  Of who she but bid follow.

Pau.   How ? not women ?

Gen. Women will love her, that she is a woman   110
  More worth than any man ; men, that she is
  The rarest of all women.

Leo.   Go, Cleomenes ;
  Yourself, assisted with your honour'd friends,

Bring them to our embracement.

Exeunt Cleomenes and others

Still, 'tis strange

He thus should steal upon us.

Pau.   Had our prince

(Jewel of children) seen this hour, he had pair'd

Well with this lord : there was not full a month

Between their births.

Leo. Prithee, no more ; cease ; thou know'st

He dies to me again, when talk'd of : sure,   120

When I shall see this gentleman, thy speeches

Will bring me to consider that which may

Unfurnish me of reason. They are come.

Re-enter Cleomenes and others, with Florizel
and Perdita

Your mother was most true to wedlock, prince ;

For she did print your royal father off,

Conceiving you : were I but twenty-one,

Your father's image is so hit in you,

His very air, that I should call you brother,

As I did him, and speak of something wildly

By us perform'd before. Most dearly welcome !   130

And your fair princess,—goddess !—O, alas !

I lost a couple, that 'twixt heaven and earth

Might thus have stood, begetting wonder, as

You, gracious couple, do : and then I lost
(All mine own folly) the society,
Amity too, of your brave father, whom,
Though bearing misery, I desire my life
Once more to look on him.

Flo.   By his command
Have I here touch'd Sicilia, and from him
Give you all greetings, that a king, at friend,   140
Can send his brother : and, but infirmity,
Which waits upon worn times, hath something seiz'd
His wish'd ability, he had himself
The lands and waters 'twixt your throne and his
Measur'd, to look upon you ; whom he loves
(He bade me say so) more than all the sceptres
And those that bear them living.

Leo.   O my brother,
Good gentleman ! the wrongs I have done thee stir
Afresh within me ; and these thy offices,
So rarely kind, are as interpreters   150
Of my behind-hand slackness !   Welcome hither,
As is the spring to the earth.   And hath he too
Expos'd this paragon to the fearful usage,
At least ungentle, of the dreadful Neptune,
To greet a man not worth her pains, much less
The adventure of her person ?

Flo.   Good my lord,
    She came from Libya.

Leo.   Where the warlike Smalus,
    That noble honour'd lord, is fear'd and lov'd?

Flo. Most royal sir, from thence; from him, whose
       daughter
    His tears proclaim'd his, parting with her: thence   160
    (A prosperous south-wind friendly) we have cross'd,
    To execute the charge my father gave me,
    For visiting your highness: my best train
    I have from your Sicilian shores dismiss'd;
    Who for Bohemia bend, to signify
    Not only my success in Libya, sir,
    But my arrival, and my wife's, in safety
    Here, where we are.

Leo.   The blessed gods
    Purge all infection from our air, whilst you
    Do climate here!   You have a holy father,   170
    A graceful gentleman, against whose person,
    So sacred as it is, I have done sin,
    For which the heavens, taking angry note,
    Have left me issueless; and your father's bless'd
    (As he from heaven merits it) with you
    Worthy his goodness.   What might I have been,
    Might I a son and daughter now have look'd on,

Such goodly things as you !

Enter a Lord

Lord.   Most noble sir,
That which I shall report will bear no credit,
Were not the proof so nigh.   Please you, great sir,   180
Bohemia greets you from himself by me ;
Desires you to attach his son, who has
(His dignity and duty both cast off)
Fled from his father, from his hopes, and with
A shepherd's daughter.

Leo.   Where 's Bohemia ? speak.

Lord. Here, in your city ; I now came from him :
I speak amazedly, and it becomes
My marvel and my message.   To your court
Whiles he was hastening (in the chase, it seems,
Of this fair couple) meets he on the way   190
The father of this seeming lady and
Her brother, having both their country quitted
With this young prince.

Flo.   Camillo has betray'd me ;
Whose honour and whose honesty till now
Endur'd all weathers.

Lord.   Lay 't so to his charge :
He 's with the king your father.

Leo.   Who ? Camillo ?

*Lord.*Camillo, sir; I spake with him; who now
    Has these poor men in question. Never saw I
    Wretches so quake: they kneel, they kiss the earth;
    Forswear themselves as often as they speak: 200
    Bohemia stops his ears, and threatens them
    With divers deaths in death.

Per.   O my poor father!
    The heaven sets spies upon us, will not have
    Our contract celebrated.

Leo.   You are married?

Flo. We are not, sir, nor are we like to be;
    The stars, I see, will kiss the valleys first:
    The odds for high and low's alike.

Leo.   My lord,
    Is this the daughter of a king?

Flo.   She is,
    When once she is my wife.

Leo. That 'once,' I see, by your good father's speed,   210
    Will come on very slowly. I am sorry,
    Most sorry, you have broken from his liking
    Where you were tied in duty, and as sorry
    Your choice is not so rich in worth as beauty,
    That you might well enjoy her.

Flo.   Dear, look up:
    Though Fortune, visible an enemy,

Should chase us, with my father, power no jot
Hath she to change our loves. Beseech you, sir,
Remember since you ow'd no more to time
Than I do now: with thought of such affections,   220
Step forth mine advocate; at your request
My father will grant precious things as trifles.

Leo. Would he do so, I 'ld beg your precious mistress,
Which he counts but a trifle.

Pau.   Sir, my liege,
Your eye hath too much youth in 't; not a month
'Fore your queen died, she was more worth such gazes
Than what you look on now.

Leo.   I thought of her,
Even in these looks I made. (*to Florizel*) But your petition
Is yet unanswer'd. I will to your father:
Your honour not o'erthrown by your desires,   230
I am friend to them and you: upon which errand
I now go toward him; therefore follow me
And mark what way I make: come, good my lord.

                                        Exeunt

SCENE II

Before Leontes' palace

Enter Autolycus and a Gentleman

Aut. Beseech you, sir, were you present at this relation?

1.G. I was by at the opening of the fardel, heard the old
shepherd deliver the manner how he found it:
whereupon, after a little amazedness, we were all
commanded out of the chamber; only this methought I heard the shepherd say, he found the child.

Aut. I would most gladly know the issue of it.

1.G. I make a broken delivery of the business; but the
changes I perceived in the king and Camillo were
very notes of admiration: they seem'd almost, with   10
staring on one another, to tear the cases of their
eyes; there was speech in their dumbness, language
in their very gesture; they look'd as they had
heard of a world ransom'd, or one destroyed: a
notable passion of wonder appeared in them; but
the wisest beholder, that knew no more but seeing,
could not say if the importance were joy, or sorrow;
but in the extremity of the one, it must needs be.

Enter another Gentleman

Here comes a gentleman that haply knows more.
The news, Rogero?   20

2.*G.* Nothing but bonfires : the oracle is fulfill'd ; the
king's daughter is found : such a deal of wonder is
broken out within this hour, that ballad-makers
cannot be able to express it.

Enter a third Gentleman

Here comes the Lady Paulina's steward, he can
deliver you more.   How goes it now, sir ? this
news (which is called true) is so like an old tale, that
the verity of it is in strong suspicion : has the king
found his heir ?

3.*G.* Most true, if ever truth were pregnant by circum-   30
stance : that which you hear you 'll swear you see,
there is such unity in the proofs.   The mantle of
Queen Hermione's ; her jewel about the neck of it ;
the letters of Antigonus found with it, which they
know to be his character ; the majesty of the creature,
in resemblance of the mother ; the affection of
nobleness, which nature shows above her breeding,
and many other evidences, proclaim her, with all
certainty, to be the king's daughter.   Did you see
the meeting of the two kings ?   40

2.*G.* No.

3.*G.* Then have you lost a sight, which was to be seen,
cannot be spoken of.   There might you have beheld
one joy crown another, so and in such manner, that

it seem'd sorrow wept to take leave of them; for
their joy waded in tears. There was casting up of
eyes, holding up of hands, with countenance of such
distraction, that they were to be known by garment,
not by favour. Our king, being ready to leap out
of himself, for joy of his found daughter, as if that 50
joy were now become a loss, cries ' O, thy mother,
thy mother!' then asks Bohemia forgiveness, then
embraces his son-in-law; then again worries he his
daughter with clipping her; now he thanks the old
shepherd, which stands by like a weather-bitten
conduit of many kings' reigns. I never heard of
such another encounter, which lames report to
follow it, and undoes description to do it.

2.*G.* What, pray you, became of Antigonus, that carried
hence the child? 60

3.*G.* Like an old tale still, which will have matter to
rehearse, though credit be asleep, and not an ear
open. He was torn to pieces with a bear: this
avouches the shepherd's son; who has not only his
innocence (which seems much) to justify him, but
a handkerchief and rings of his, that Paulina knows.

1.*G.* What became of his bark, and his followers?

3.*G.* Wreck'd the same instant of their master's death,
and in the view of the shepherd: so that all the

instruments which aided to expose the child were   70
even then lost, when it was found.   But O, the
noble combat that 'twixt joy and sorrow was fought
in Paulina !   She had one eye declin'd for the loss of
her husband, another elevated, that the oracle was
fulfill'd : she lifted the princess from the earth, and
so locks her in embracing, as if she would pin her to
her heart, that she might no more be in danger of
losing.

1.G. The dignity of this act was worth the audience of
kings and princes, for by such was it acted.   80

3.G. One of the prettiest touches of all, and that which
angled for mine eyes (caught the water though not
the fish) was when at the relation of the queen's
death (with the manner how she came to 't bravely
confessed and lamented by the king) how attentive-
ness wounded his daughter, till, from one sign of
dolour to another, she did, with an ' Alas,' I would
fain say, bleed tears ; for I am sure my heart wept
blood.   Who was most marble, there chang'd
colour ; some swounded, all sorrowed : if all the   90
world could have seen 't, the woe had been
universal.

1.G. Are they returned to the court ?

3.G. No : the princess hearing of her mother's statue,

which is in the keeping of Paulina,—a piece many years in doing, and now newly perform'd, by that rare Italian master, Julio Romano, who (had he himself eternity, and could put breath into his work) would beguile Nature of her custom, so perfectly he is her ape : he so near to Hermione hath done 100 Hermione, that they say one would speak to her, and stand in hope of answer :—thither with all greediness of affection are they gone, and there they intend to sup.

2.G. I thought she had some great matter there in hand, for she hath privately twice or thrice a day, ever since the death of Hermione, visited that removed house. Shall we thither, and with our company piece the rejoicing ?

1.G. Who would be thence, that has the benefit of 110 access ? every wink of an eye, some new grace will be born : our absence makes us unthrifty to our knowledge. Let's along. *Exeunt Gentlemen*

Aut. Now, had I not the dash of my former life in me, would preferment drop on my head. I brought the old man and his son aboard the prince ; told him I heard them talk of a fardel, and I know not what : but he at that time overfond of the shepherd's daughter (so he then took her to be) who began to

be much sea-sick, and himself little better, extremity 120
of weather continuing, this mystery remained un-
discover'd. But 'tis all one to me; for had I been
the finder out of this secret, it would not have
relish'd among my other discredits.

Enter Shepherd and Clown

Here comes those I have done good to against my
will, and already appearing in the blossoms of their
fortune.

She. Come, boy, I am past moe children; but thy sons
and daughters will be all gentlemen born.

Clo. You are well met, sir.   You denied to fight with me 130
this other day, because I was no gentleman born.
See you these clothes? say you see them not, and
think me still no gentleman born: you were best
say these robes are not gentleman born: give me the
lie; do; and try whether I am not now a gentleman
born.

Aut. I know you are now, sir, a gentleman born.

Clo. Ay, and have been so any time these four hours.

She. And so have I, boy.

Clo. So you have: but I was a gentleman born before 140
my father; for the king's son took me by the hand,
and called me brother; and then the two kings

133

call'd my father brother; and then the prince (my
brother) and the princess (my sister) call'd my
father father; and so we wept; and there was
the first gentleman-like tears that ever we shed.

She. We may live, son, to shed many more.

Clo. Ay; or else 'twere hard luck, being in so preposter-
ous estate as we are.

Aut. I humbly beseech you, sir, to pardon me all the faults 150
I have committed to your worship, and to give me
your good report to the prince my master.

She. Prithee, son, do; for we must be gentle, now we are
gentlemen.

Clo. Thou wilt amend thy life?

Aut. Ay, an it like your good worship.

Clo. Give me thy hand: I will swear to the prince thou
art as honest a true fellow as any is in Bohemia.

She. You may say it, but not swear it.

Clo. Not swear it, now I am a gentleman? Let boors 160
and franklins say it, I'll swear it.

She. How if it be false, son?

Clo. If it be ne'er so false, a true gentleman may swear
it, in the behalf of his friend: and I'll swear to the
prince thou art a tall fellow of thy hands, and that
thou wilt not be drunk; but I know thou art no
tall fellow of thy hands, and that thou wilt be drunk:

134

but I 'll swear it, and I would thou wouldst be a tall
fellow of thy hands.

Aut. I will prove so, sir, to my power.   170

Clo. Ay, by any means prove a tall fellow : if I do not
wonder how thou dar'st venture to be drunk, not
being a tall fellow, trust me not.   Hark !   the kings
and the princes (our kindred) are going to see the
queen's picture.   Come, follow us : we 'll be thy
good masters.   *Exeunt*

SCENE III

A chapel in Paulina's house

Enter Leontes, Polixenes, Florizel, Perdita, Camillo,
Paulina, Lords, and Attendants

Leo. O grave and good Paulina, the great comfort
That I have had of thee !

Pau.   What, sovereign sir,
I did not well, I meant well : all my services
You have paid home.   But that you have vouchsaf'd
With your crown'd brother, and these your contracted
Heirs of your kingdoms, my poor house to visit,
It is a surplus of your grace, which never
My life may last to answer.

Leo.   O Paulina,
We honour you with trouble : but we came
To see the statue of our queen : your gallery   10
Have we pass'd through, not without much content
In many singularities ; but we saw not
That which my daughter came to look upon,
The statue of her mother.

Pau.   As she liv'd peerless,
So her dead likeness, I do well believe,
Excels whatever yet you look'd upon,
Or hand of man hath done ; therefore I keep it
Lonely, apart.   But here it is : prepare
To see the life as lively mock'd as ever
Still sleep mock'd death : behold, and say 'tis well.   20

    Paulina draws a curtain, and discovers
     Hermione standing like a statue

I like your silence, it the more shows off
Your wonder : but yet speak ; first, you, my liege,
Comes it not something near ?

Leo.   Her natural posture !
Chide me, dear stone, that I may say indeed
Thou art Hermione ; or rather, thou art she
In thy not chiding, for she was as tender
As infancy and grace.   But yet, Paulina,
Hermione was not so much wrinkled, nothing

So aged as this seems.

Pol.   O, not by much.

Pau. So much the more our carver's excellence;   30
   Which lets go by some sixteen years, and makes her
   As she liv'd now.

Leo.   As now she might have done,
   So much to my good comfort, as it is
   Now piercing to my soul.   O, thus she stood,
   Even with such life of majesty (warm life,
   As now it coldly stands) when first I woo'd her!
   I am asham'd: does not the stone rebuke me,
   For being more stone than it?   O royal piece;
   There's magic in thy majesty, which has
   My evils conjur'd to remembrance;   and   40
   From thy admiring daughter took the spirits,
   Standing like stone with thee.

Per.   And give me leave,
   And do not say 'tis superstition, that
   I kneel, and then implore her blessing.   Lady,
   Dear queen, that ended when I but began,
   Give me that hand of yours, to kiss.

Pau.   O, patience!
   The statue is but newly fix'd, the colour's
   Not dry.

Cam. My lord, your sorrow was too sore laid on,

137

    Which sixteen winters cannot blow away,   50
    So many summers dry : scarce any joy
    Did ever so long live ; no sorrow
    But kill'd itself much sooner.

Pol.   Dear my brother,
    Let him that was the cause of this have power
    To take off so much grief from you as he
    Will piece up in himself.

Pau.   Indeed, my lord,
    If I had thought the sight of my poor image
    Would thus have wrought you (for the stone is
        mine)
    I 'ld not have show'd it.

Leo.   Do not draw the curtain.

Pau. No longer shall you gaze on 't, lest your fancy   60
    May think anon, it moves.

Leo.   Let be, let be.
    Would I were dead, but that, methinks, already—
    What was he that did make it ?   See, my lord,
    Would you not deem it breath'd ? and that those veins
    Did verily bear blood ?

Pol.   Masterly done :
    The very life seems warm upon her lip.

Leo. The fixure of her eye has motion in 't,
    As we are mock'd with art.

Pau.   I 'll draw the curtain :
My lord 's almost so far transported that
He 'll think anon it lives.

Leo.   O sweet Paulina,   70
Make me to think so twenty years together !
No settled senses of the world can match
The pleasure of that madness.   Let 't alone.

Pau. I am sorry, sir, I have thus far stirr'd you : but
I could afflict you farther.

Leo.   Do, Paulina ;
For this affliction has a taste as sweet
As any cordial comfort.   Still, methinks,
There is an air comes from her : what fine chisel
Could ever yet cut breath ?   Let no man mock me,
For I will kiss her.

Pau.   Good my lord, forbear :   80
The ruddiness upon her lip is wet ;
You 'll mar it, if you kiss it, stain your own
With oily painting.   Shall I draw the curtain ?

Leo. No, not these twenty years.

Per.   So long could I
Stand by, a looker on.

Pau.   Either forbear,
Quit presently the chapel, or resolve you
For more amazement.   If you can behold it,

I 'll make the statue move indeed ; descend,
And take you by the hand : but then you 'll think
(Which I protest against) I am assisted   90
By wicked powers.

Leo.   What you can make her do,
I am content to look on : what to speak,
I am content to hear ; for 'tis as easy
To make her speak as move.

Pau.   It is requir'd
You do awake your faith.   Then, all stand still ;
Or those that think it is unlawful business   †
I am about, let them depart.

Leo.   Proceed :
No foot shall stir.

Pau.   Music awake her ; strike !   *Music*
'Tis time ; descend ; be stone no more ; approach ;
Strike all that look upon with marvel.   Come ;   100
I 'll fill your grave up : stir ; nay, come away ;
Bequeath to death your numbness, for from him
Dear life redeems you.   You perceive she stirs :

                              Hermione comes down

Start not ; her actions shall be holy, as
You hear my spell is lawful : do not shun her,
Until you see her die again ; for then
You kill her double.   Nay, present your hand :

When she was young, you woo'd her ; now, in age,
Is she become the suitor ?

Leo.   O, she 's warm !
If this be magic, let it be an art   110
Lawful as eating.

Pol.   She embraces him.

Cam. She hangs about his neck,
If she pertain to life, let her speak too.

Pol. Ay, and mak 't manifest where she has lived,
Or how stolen from the dead.

Pau.   That she is living,
Were it but told you, should be hooted at
Like an old tale : but it appears she lives,
Though yet she speak not.   Mark a little while :
Please you to interpose, fair madam : kneel,
And pray your mother's blessing : turn, good lady, 120
Our Perdita is found.

Her.   You gods, look down,
And from your sacred vials pour your graces
Upon my daughter's head ! Tell me, mine own,
Where hast thou been preserv'd ? where liv'd ? how
      found
Thy father's court ? for thou shalt hear that I,
Knowing by Paulina that the oracle
Gave hope thou wast in being, have preserv'd

Myself to see the issue.

Pau.   There 's time enough for that,
Lest they desire upon this push to trouble
Your joys with like relation.   Go together,   130
You precious winners all ; your exultation
Partake to every one.   I (an old turtle)
Will wing me to some wither'd bough, and there
My mate, that 's never to be found again,
Lament, till I am lost.

Leo.   O, peace, Paulina !
Thou shouldst a husband take by my consent,
As I by thine a wife : this is a match,
And made between 's by vows.   Thou hast found
        mine,
But how, is to be question'd ; for I saw her,
As I thought, dead ; and have (in vain) said many   140
A prayer upon her grave.   I 'll not seek far
(For him, I partly know his mind) to find thee
An honourable husband.   Come, Camillo,
And take her by the hand ; whose worth and honesty
Is richly noted, and here justified
By us, a pair of kings.   Let 's from this place.
What ? look upon my brother : both your pardons, †
That e'er I put between your holy looks
My ill suspicion.   This your son-in law,

And son unto the king, whom heavens directing,   150
Is troth-plight to your daughter.   Good Paulina,
Lead us from hence, where we may leisurely
Each one demand, and answer to his part
Perform'd in this wide gap of time, since first
We were dissever'd : hastily lead away.   *Exeunt*

Notes

I. i. 74-75. *the imposition* . . .; *i.e.* we could have cleared ourselves even of the charge of 'original sin.'

I. ii. 11. *I am question'd by my fears* . . .; a much disputed passage. The reading of the text implies a sense which is a development of that put forward by Hanmer. It is the reading of F with the insertion of the brackets, and the passage would mean 'I am afraid of what conspiracy may breed in my absence, which may come to full bloom if there is no nipping wind to prevent it, and then we shall have to say that it is too true a bloom of conspiracy.' On this interpretation the key is that *blow* is used as of a flower, not as of a wind. I should feel more happy about it if it were more natural to use *sneaping* in a semi-complimentary sense.

I. ii. 96. *beat an acre*; there is, I think, clearly some corruption. N.E.D. doubtfully suggests for *beat* ' to run swiftly over, as in a race,' but even if this meaning were tenable, *acre* is very awkward, since what is wanted is a measure of length and not of area, and of a short length at that.

I. ii. 138. *Affection?* . . .; the sense of this obscure passage seems to be ' if the mental purpose roused by physical instinct can give reality to mere fancy, *a fortiori* it can be dominant when there is some reality for it to take hold on.'

I. ii. 324. *I have lov'd thee*; the New Cambridge editors rightly point out that it is most unlikely that Camillo would address the king as *thee*; they would therefore read *T' have lov'd the*—, which is easy enough graphically, but it is not particularly good in sense, nor does it seem to give much of a point of departure for Leontes' retort.

I. ii. 458. *Good expedition . . .*; this has caused much trouble, and many editors accept Warburton's emendation *queen's*; but Malone's view that *comfort* is a verb is probably right and gives adequate sense. *Nothing of* means ' no (legitimate) part of.'

II. i. 134. *I'll keep my stables . . .*; the sense is clear from the phrase that follows. Antigonus must mean that he will keep his wife under the closest observation. But why it should mean that no one has adequately explained. Is it just that he will keep her as it were in a stall? Cf. *Much Ado about Nothing*, III. iv. 44.

II. i. 143. *land-damn*; F *Land-damne*. No satisfactory explanation. It looks like a repetition of *damn'd* in the line before with an intensive prefix, though it may be, as some editors think, no more than a coined word meaning to thrash, ' lambast.'

II. i. 153. *doing thus*; there must here be some stage business. Capell thought that Leontes pulled Antigonus' nose (a sign of contempt for a person's wits), which seems as probable as anything else.

II. iii. 159. *Lady Margery*; the New Cambridge editors acutely point out that as ' margery-prater' was slang for a hen, *Lady Margery* is a variant on *Dame Partlet* above.

III. i. (S.D.). I borrow the stage-direction from the New Cambridge editors, who rightly point out that at the end of the last scene the two emissaries are reported as already posting to the court, so that the traditional ' a seaport ' will not do.

III. i. 2. *isle*; Shakespeare takes over from Greene the confusion between Delos, the island sacred to Apollo, and Delphi, where his oracle was.

III. ii. 49. *With what encounter . . .*; ' with what kind of unsanctioned behaviour I have gone beyond due bounds so that I appear in this light.'

III. ii. 59-61. *More than mistress of . . .*; though the sense is clear, I doubt whether it can be wrested from the words as they stand, and to quote ' more mirth than I am mistress of' from *As You Like It*, though it makes clear what was hardly obscure, that Hermione is picking up Leontes' *own it*, is not otherwise helpful. Hermione means that she must not acknowledge any guilty implications of her actions.

III. iii. 1. Shakespeare again follows Greene into error and on to the famous sea-coast of Bohemia.

III. iii. 58. *S.D.*; one of the very few stage-directions in this text. There can be no reasonable doubt that the bear appeared on the stage. *Mucedorus* was revived in 1610 or 1611 (probably the latter) with a scene specially written for a clown and a white bear; and two white bears drew a chariot in Jonson's masque *Oberon* (1611). It looks as though about this time there was a favourite (and well-trained) bear available, as much of a draw, one may imagine, as a star film-dog.

III. iii. 74. *trunk-work*; *i.e.* the kind of trick by which Iachimo secures access to Imogen.

III. iii. 98. *flap-dragoned*; *i.e.* swallowed, from a game apparently like the modern snap-dragon, in which raisins in burning brandy were extinguished by being taken in the mouth.

IV. iii. 7. *pugging*; since ' puggard' was slang for a thief, there is no need to take Collier's emendation ' prigging' (with the same sense), though it is graphically easy enough.

IV. iii. 23. *My traffic is sheets . . .*; Charlton explains that this means that when the kite builds its nest people must look after small articles which the kite may take as material, but that Autolycus is after bigger game. And there is doubtless an allusion to the practice of the thieves who with a hook on the end of a long stick pulled down from windows articles there hung out. I would feel happier about the explanation if the order of the clauses in the text were transposed, and *My traffic is sheets* were the climax.

IV. iii. 25. Shakespeare's Autolycus is only born ' under Mercury.' The classical Autolycus was Mercury's son, and so a hereditary thief, ' such a fellow as in theft and filching had no peer,' as Golding's translation of the *Metamorphoses* describes him.

IV. iii. 51. *I' the name of me !*; there has been a deal of needless bother about this, many editors taking *me* to be an incompleted *mercy*. It is merely a euphemism, like ''Fore me!' for ''Fore God!', though it has a comic turn and may well have been intended as a comment on the edict to restrain swearing on the stage.

IV. iv. 9. *swain's wearing*; no doubt Florizel's wearing may be a kind of fancy dress, but there can surely be no doubt that Perdita means that whereas she has been, in both senses, dressed up, he has been dressed down. The point is of some importance, because attempts have been made to show that Florizel's apparel is so ' fancy ' that it can later be naturally mistaken for that of a courtier. It is so mistaken, but why is difficult to understand.

IV. iv. 13. *sworn*; the New Cambridge editors support Theobald's reading *swoon*. If one could agree that Perdita ' is evidently in great agitation at the opening of this scene ' one would accept the emendation with readier alacrity. But I cannot see that she is more than rather pleasurably fluttered, and *swoon* is a strong word. It is graphically easy, and gives a good balance. If F's reading is retained it must mean, I think, that Florizel by his attire is reminding Perdita of what she really is, *i.e.* the shepherdess.

IV. iv. 79-85. Perdita's trouble is that she dislikes the autumn (middle-aged) flowers which would suit them, and so has to approximate with winter flowers. Both carnations and gillyflowers were traditionally connected with wantonness.

IV. iv. 104. *Hot*; mysterious. No one has explained why lavender should be hot. The New Cambridge editors suggest *Goat*, in the sense of 'wild' (*cf.* goat-marjoram), but they do not explain why the lavender should be wild when everything else is from Perdita's garden.

IV. iv. 119. *take*; it seems almost impiety to annotate one of the loveliest of famous passages; but it is easy to miss the force of *take*. It can, of course, mean just 'captivate' (as in the modern 'to be taken with'); but it had also a much stronger meaning, 'to enchant' (usually malignantly, as in 'no fairy takes, nor witch hath power to charm'). The winds of March are not only captivated; they are quelled.

IV. iv. 195. *dildos and fadings*; contradicting the *so without bawdry*, since *dildo* is common in ballad refrains for the phallus, and *fading* is part of 'the refrain of a popular song of indecent character' (N.E.D., not further explained).

IV. iv. 246. *clammer*; a technical term in bell-ringing, for the acceleration of the strokes leading up to the final stoppage.

IV. iv. 248. *tawdry-lace*; a corruption of 'St Audrey lace'; the saint died of a tumour in the throat which she regarded as punishment for a vain love of necklaces in her youth.

IV. iv. 438-39. *Even here undone! I was not...*; F reads *Even heere undone: I was not...*: and a colon is not uncommon for an exclamation mark. The New Cambridge editors adopt with admiration Johnson's punctuation, *Even here, undone, I was not...*, and blame all other editors for not explaining the 'pointless exclamation' of the text. But why is the exclamation pointless? When Perdita's castle in the air has suddenly fallen in fragments about her ears, is not *Even here undone !* as natural a remark as might be? *I was not much afeard* seems to me on any showing a curious remark, but Johnson's punctuation only partially helps it. I fancy that Perdita's remark is one of puzzlement. She feels that she naturally should have been *afeard* before the king—she has been true to her blood, and felt, to her own surprise, like a king's daughter.

IV. iv. 740. *pheasant*; unless this is corrupt, which there is no reason to suppose, the New Cambridge editors are surely right in seeing an allusion to the custom of bribing magistrates with a bird, *cf.* ' capon justices.'

V. ii. 97. *Julio Romano*; a famous Italian painter who died in 1546. He also practised sculpture.

V. iii. 96. *Or those that think . . .*; Hanmer's attractive emendation of F's *On : those that think.*

V. iii. 147. *What ? look upon my brother*; it is tempting to insert a stage-direction here. The point of the remark is usually explained in such terms as ' Uttered as he suddenly catches sight of Polixenes, and forgets that he has been leaving him out of it.' The point is surely much sharper and more ironic than that. Polixenes and Hermione, as I take it, are, not unnaturally, a little ill at ease, remembering the last time that they looked at each other, and Hermione is rather consciously *not* looking at Polixenes. Leontes gives her, but in a very different spirit, as direct a command as his *Tongue-tied, our queen ? speak you* of I. ii.

Glossary

MANY words and phrases in Shakespeare require glossing, not because they are in themselves unfamiliar, but for the opposite reason, that Shakespeare uses in their Elizabethan and unfamiliar sense a large number of words which seem so familiar that there is no incentive to look for them in the glossary. It is hoped that a glossary arranged as below will make it easy to see at a glance what words and phrases in any particular scene require elucidation. A number of phrases are glossed by what seems to be, in their context, the modern equivalent rather than by lexicographical glosses on the words which compose them.

Act First

SCENE I

line
6 BOHEMIA, *sc.* the King of
27 ATTORNEYED, proxied
30 VAST, chasm

line
37 NOTE, notice
39 PHYSICS, vitalises
SUBJECT, subjects

SCENE II

1 WATERY STAR, moon
1-2 HATH BEEN THE SHEPHERD'S NOTE, the shepherd has noticed
6 CIPHER, nought (the figure)
8 MOE, more (*Eliz. plur.*)
18 I'LL, I'll have
33 WARD, guard (*fencing*)
41 LET, *either* hinder *or* allow to stay
GEST, time allotted for stage or halt in journey

42 PREFIX'D, fixed beforehand
43 JAR, tick
46 LIMBER, limp
51 YET, none the less
81 OF THIS MAKE NO CONCLUSION, don't carry this to its logical conclusion
93 THAT, *i.e.* its happening
112 LIBERTY, license
118 MORT, death (*i.e.* final surrender)

151

Act I Sc. ii—*continued*

line

121 BAWCOCK, 'stout fellow'

125 VIRGINALLING, playing (as **on a** keyboard)

128 PASH, head (*dial.*)

132 O'ER-DYED BLACKS, too often dyed (and so worn-out) black garments

136 WELKIN, sky (*i.e.* blue)

137 COLLOP, *lit.* slice: *i.e.* chip of the old block

144 COMMISSION, instruction

146 HARDENING OF MY BROWS, *i.e.* with the cuckold's horns

155 UNBREECH'D, still in petticoats

156 MUZZLED, with the 'button' on, 'bated'

160 SQUASH, unripe peascod

161 TAKE EGGS FOR MONEY, 'be put off with something worthless' (*trad. phrase, orig. unknown*)

163 HAPPY MAN BE'S DOLE, properly good luck to you (*here exactly* 'attaboy')

166 EXERCISE, care
    MATTER, thoughts

168 PARASITE, hanger-on

171-2 SO STANDS . . . OFFIC'D, has the same status

177 APPARENT, next in succession

183 NEB, nose ('*to neb*'='*to bill*' in the '*bill and coo*' sense)

184 ARMS, links arms

186 FORK'D ONE, *i.e.* cuckold

line

194 SLUIC'D, *met. from draining water off from fish-pond by sluice-gates*

201 STRIKE, affect malignantly

217 THEY'RE HERE WITH ME, 'they're on to it'
    ROUNDING, whispering

219 GUST, taste

224 CONCEIT, understanding
    SOAKING, *i.e.* quick in the uptake

225 BLOCKS, heads

226 SEVERALS, individuals

227 MESS, group of diners (*so here* '*lower messes*'=the lower orders)

242 BIDE UPON'T, reiterate
    HONEST, honourable

244 HOXES, hamstrings

246 GRAFTED IN, admitted to

248 DRAWN, won

254 PUTS FORTH, appears

263 ALLOW'D, recognised

268 EYE-GLASS, eye (lens of)

270 APPARENT, keen

274 IMPUDENTLY, shamelessly

276 HOBBY-HORSE, prostitute

277 RANK, coarse
    FLAX-WENCH, flax-worker (as type of low woman)
    PUTS TO, copulates

284 THOUGH, even if

291 THE PIN AND WEB, (*roughly*) cataract

Act I Sc. ii—*continued*

line

302 HOVERING, wavering

306 GLASS, hour-glass

314 BENCH'D, raised to seat of dignity

REAR'D, raised

317 WINK, sleep

326 APPOINT, put

330 GIVE SCANDAL TO THE BLOOD, question the legitimacy

333 BLENCH, swerve

334 FETCH OFF, ' remove '

338 INJURY, scandalous talk

344 KEEP, keep on good terms with

372 FALLING, letting fall

374 BREEDING, maturing

378 BE INTELLIGENT TO, make it clear to

line

378 'TIS THEREABOUTS, this is how it stands

388 SIGHTED LIKE THE BASILISK, with eyes like the basilisk (*serpent supposed to kill with glance of eye*)

393 GENTRY, gentle breeding

394 IN WHOSE SUCCESS, by descent from whom

416 VICE, force (*with pun on sense of wickedness*)

419 THAT DID BETRAY THE BEST, *i.e.* Judas

435 TRUNK, body (*perhaps with pun*)

436 IMPAWN'D, as security

Act Second

SCENE I

25 SAD, serious

37 CENSURE, judgment

45 HEFTS, retchings

51 PINCH'D, trapped

90 FEDERARY, accomplice

102 CENTRE, earth (as centre of universe)

105 BUT THAT HE SPEAKS, merely by his speaking

141 PUTTER-ON, inciter

149 GLIB, castrate

165 OR, either

170 PROPERLY, peculiarly

172 OVERTURE, disclosure

182 POST, haste

185 STUFF'D SUFFICIENCY, full reliability

SCENE II

30 LUNES, freaks

47 PRESENTLY, at once

49 HAMMER'D OF, deliberated on

50 TEMPT, try

SCENE III

Act Third

SCENE I

SCENE II

SCENE III

Act III Sc. iii—*continued*

<table>
<tr><td>line</td><td></td></tr>
<tr><td>41 BE SQUAR'D, behave accordingly</td><td>115 BEARING-CLOTH, christening-robe</td></tr>
<tr><td>47 CHARACTER, description</td><td>SQUIRE, gentleman next below a knight</td></tr>
<tr><td>70 BARNE, child
CHILD, girl</td><td>124 NEXT, nearest</td></tr>
<tr><td>72 SCAPE, 'slip'</td><td>130 CURST, dangerous</td></tr>
</table>

Act Fourth

SCENE I

18 FOND, foolish

SCENE II

46 ANGLE, bait on hook

SCENE III

2 DOXY, beggar's drab	43 MEANS, tenors
4 PALE, pallor	46 WARDEN, of Warden pears
14 THREE-PILE, rich velvet	47 RACE, root
20 BUDGET, wallet	49 RAISINS O' THE SUN, sun-dried grapes (*i.e. simply* raisins)
26-27 WITH DIE AND DRAB I PURCHAS'D THIS CAPARISON, dicing and drabbing have brought me to these rags	86 TROLL-MY-DAMES, game like bagatelle played by ladies (*and ? hence* the players themselves)
28 KNOCK, blows	94 APE-BEARER, 'organ-grinder'
32 'LEVEN WETHER TOD, 28 lbs. of wool (yielded by 11 sheep)	PROCESS SERVER, writ-server
35 SPRINGE, trap	95 COMPASS'D A MOTION, got hold of a puppet-show
COCK, woodcock (*traditionally foolish bird*)	98 IN, into the part of
42 THREE-MAN SONG-MEN, singers of 3-part songs	100 PRIG, thief
	101 WAKE, annual parish festival

THE WINTER'S TALE

SCENE IV

line
1 WEEDS, clothes
3 PEERING, peeping
8 MARK, cynosure
11 MESS, group of diners
23 FLAUNTS, 'plumes'
24 APPREHEND, imagine
41 FORC'D, far-fetched
42 OR, either
74 ROSEMARY, *for remembrance*
RUE, *for repentance*
75 SEEMING, beauty
SAVOUR, scent
89 MEAN, means
114 BECOME, suit
116 PROSERPINA, Prŏserpĭna
118 DIS, *i.e.* Pluto, the king of hell
127 FLOWER-DE-LUCE, iris
132 QUICK, alive
143 EACH YOUR DOING, your every action
144 SINGULAR, individual
152 SKILL, reason
154 TURTLES, turtle-doves
169 FEEDING, rearing
182 TABOR, drum
196 STRETCH-MOUTH'D, loose-mouthed
197 BREAK A FOUL GAP INTO THE MATTER, insert an indecent interlude
203 UNBRAIDED, unsoiled
207 INKLES, tapes
CADDISSES, worsted garters

line
207 LAWNS, fine linens
210 SLEEVE-HAND, cuff
SQUARE, embroidered yoke
219 CYPRESS, crape
224 QUOIFS, headdresses
STOMACHERS, ornamental coverings for chest
226 POKING-STICKS, metal sticks heated and used to adjust pleats of ruff
242 PLACKET, hole in petticoat
244 KILN-HOLE, furnace-room (*for drying grain, malt, etc.*)
248 TAWDRY-LACE, silk tie
250 COZEN'D, cheated
256 CHARGE, value
263 CARBONADOED, slashed for broiling
271 MOE, more (*Eliz. plur.*)
308 SAD, serious
323 NEAT-HERDS, cow-herds
326 GALLIMAUFRY, jumble
328 BOWLING, playing bowls
336 JUMPS, *i.e.* the caper in morris-dancing
350 INTERPRETATION SHOULD ABUSE, should misinterpret you
361 BOLTED, sifted
396 ALTERING RHEUMS, rheumatism which transforms him
403 REASON, it is reasonable that
423 FOND, foolish
425 KNACK, trinket

156

Act IV Sc. iv—*continued*

line		line	
428	FARRE, farther	604	PETTITOES, trotters
	DEUCALION, the 'Noah' of Greek mythology	676	CLOG, encumbrance
		704	FARDEL, bundle
479	FANCY, love	711	EXCREMENT, outgrowth
511	CURIOUS, demanding care	732	TOAZE, elicit
595	POMANDER, scent-ball	766	IN HAND-FAST, under arrest
	TABLE-BOOK, memorandum-book	814	CASE, casing (*with pun*)
		821	PAWN, hostage

Act Fifth

SCENE I

90	OUT OF CIRCUMSTANCE, unceremonious	170	CLIMATE, reside
108	PROFESSORS, sectaries	230	YOUR HONOUR NOT, so long as your honour is not
140	AT FRIEND, as a friend		

SCENE II

10	NOTES OF ADMIRATION, exclamation marks	96	PERFORM'D, finished
		107	REMOVED, remote
17	IMPORTANCE, import	112	UNTHRIFTY, not careful to increase
36-37	AFFECTION OF NOBLENESS, unconscious nobility	116	ABOARD THE PRINCE, aboard the prince's ship
54	CLIPPING, embracing		
62	CREDIT BE ASLEEP, there is none to believe it	128	MOE, more (*Eliz. plur.*)
		161	FRANKLINS, yeomen
65	INNOCENCE, simpleness	165	TALL, 'stout'

SCENE III

4	HOME, in full	41	ADMIRING, wondering
12	SINGULARITIES, rarities	129	PUSH, occasion